NEW CONGREGATIONS

NEW CONGREGATIONS

SECURITY AND MISSION IN CONFLICT

by
Donald L. Metz

WITH A FOREWORD

by
Charles Y. Glock

THE WESTMINSTER PRESS
PHILADELPHIA

A publication from the Research Program in the Sociology of Religion, Survey Research Center, University of California, Berkeley.

Library of Congress Catalog Card No. 67–10276

PUBLISHED BY THE WESTMINSTER PRESS ®
PHILADELPHIA, PENNSYLVANIA

PRINTED IN THE UNITED STATES OF AMERICA

To My Parents
whose patience and confidence
have been a source of constant encouragement

CONTENTS

FOREWORD

Each year, America gives birth to hundreds of new churches. They come to dot the landscape of the countryside and village, the town and the city. Launched as they are out of the deep conviction of a few or of many, each begins its life with aspirations of high accomplishment. Some of these churches fail to survive. They flower briefly, only to die. Most live on—barely, comfortably, or affluently—to affect their members and their neighborhoods.

From one religious perspective, what course a church follows—whether it succeeds, fails, or falls somewhere in between—is a mystery to be understood only by God. Indeed, the very matter of judging success or failure is likely to be seen as God's business, and not man's. Yet, even among those who subscribe to such views—and perhaps, because they care, particularly among them—the uneasy feeling is likely to be generated that churches rarely turn out quite as God intended.

This book was stimulated by such an uneasy feeling. Its perspective, however, unlike the one just described, is that it is appropriate to ask and possible to learn how and why new churches evolve as they do. Like human beings, churches are inexorably caught up in their environments, and in subtle ways environments exercise an influence on institutional as well as on human growth. Learning what these influences are will not entirely account for the process of growth. Yet, understanding them seems important if institutions and human beings are to meet their potentials. With respect specifically to churches, knowledge of what produces the gap between what churches aspire to and what they accomplish seems a prerequisite to narrowing the gap and eventually perhaps to closing it.

The reader will want to decide for himself how much his understanding of new church development is illuminated by this book. From this observer's viewpoint—and I speak both as a sociologist and as a churchman—the illumination is considerable. The book demonstrates how churches may come to be derailed from their high purposes. The description of this derailment as grounded in commitments to sheer survival makes common sense as well as scientific sense. The study is important, however, not only for what it reveals about the fundamental dilemma new churches face in accommodating their formal goals—that is, their high aspirations—to their goal of survival, but also for what it has to say about resolutions of that dilemma. As the book is careful to point out, the derailment process is not an inevitable one. Churches can and do succeed in transcending it. The experience of one church, thoughtfully examined by the author, demonstrates how this may be done.

This is a book, then, which ought to be equally rewarding to the professional sociologist concerned to understand the operation of the church in American society and to the churchman concerned to make the church a more effective force in that society.

CHARLES Y. GLOCK

PREFACE

This essay is intended to present a picture of new Protestant congregations in American society. It is based on a study that was designed to suggest hypotheses about the factors affecting the course of development of new churches. The study was conducted under a grant from the Institute of Strategic Studies of The United Presbyterian Church U.S.A., by the Survey Research Center, University of California, Berkeley.

The data upon which the empirical sections of the essay are based were gathered in the summer of 1964. They include a series of depth interviews, responses to a prior Institute questionnaire, congregational statistics from the General Assembly *Minutes*, and data on the parish areas from the United States Census of 1960. The interviews varied from one to two and a half hours in length, and were conducted separately with the organizing minister and at least six knowledgeable persons from each of six congregations. The interviewees served both as respondents in reporting their own opinions and experiences, and as informants in describing their congregations at different stages. Care was taken to ensure that the interviewees were not part of a single clique in any of the congregations but, rather, represented a variety of viewpoints. The data that were gathered through the interviews were qualitative in character and deal with a broad range of topics related to the goals, procedures, motives, atmosphere, and conditions of the congregations and their members.

In its final form this essay is a scheme of generalizations based on a subjective reading of the data. The conclusions that it contains are suggestions or hypotheses about what is happening in new congregations. The chief argument for the accuracy of the conclusions is the consistency with which they applied from case to case. Wider and more rigorous testing of them will be necessary before they can be considered adequately validated.

The essay consists of three sections. The first (Chapters 2 and 3) deals with the conceptual framework that is employed; the second and third are an analysis of the congregations at two stages of their development. Chapters 4 and 5 treat the "developing" congregation, while Chapters 6 and 7 deal with the "developed" congregation. Chapter 8 presents a congregation that is "deviant" in that its development differed significantly from the others. It is a concrete example of at least one alternative available to the congregation as an operating system. Finally, Chapter 9 provides a generalized summary of the findings in terms that are relevant to the sociological theory of organizations.

There are many persons who have made valuable contributions to the work that has gone into this book. Above all, I wish to express my appreciation to Dr. Charles Y. Glock, Director of the Survey Research Center, whose guidance was felt at every stage of the process. Dr. Everett L. Perry, Associate Chairman in charge of research and survey, Institute of Strategic Studies, provided wise and helpful counsel throughout the conduct of the study. Dr. Robert G. Holloway, of the Industrial Relations Center of the University of Chicago, and Prof. Charles S. McCoy, of the Pacific School of Religion, helped greatly with their interest and sound advice. Parker J. Palmer, of Beloit College, formerly Director of the Bureau of Community Research in Berkeley, was a valued source of solid criticism and cheerful encouragement. My wife, Mary, has contributed to this work both by her understanding nature and by her aid in many undramatic but necessary tasks of publication. To these, and to the ministers and church members who contributed some of their time and energy in the hope that this study would in some small way be of benefit to society, the author is deeply grateful.

D. L. M.

Berkeley, California

1

INTRODUCTION

If the church had been listed in the stock market over the past few decades, it would have been considered a booming enterprise. As an organization it has had an impressive growth, evident both in the enlargement of its membership and in the increasing amount of real property it controls. This expansion has found expression particularly in the founding of new congregations—congregations made necessary by a general growth of the population and by a considerable shift from rural to urban areas. The pressure for new congregations has been so heavy in recent years that denominations have been forced to reorganize their agencies and programs that deal with new church development.

The denominations' concern with new church development has not been a result merely of the quantity of new congregations; it has also sprung from the recognition that these congregations must face conditions that are significantly different from those of more established churches. In the main, the differences in conditions are the result of the spread of tract housing developments. Where churches once rose in the midst of slowly growing sectors of towns or cities, they are now springing up in what are essentially new towns, shaped out of empty land, and without traditions or forebears.

This suburban frontier on which most of the new congregations are located is a mixed blessing. On the one hand, it offers the opportunity for a new start, the possibility of establishing a congregational life that is not hindered by commitments to outmoded programs and procedures. On the other hand, the new suburb lacks the characteristics of an established community; it is usually deficient in informal social contacts, in internal communications, in stability of residents, in a sense of its own unity. As a result the new congregation must take shape in a tension between the pursuit of a fresh vision and the search for a firm foundation among the uncertainties of a new community.

Curiosity, if nothing else, should move us to wonder how the new congregations are responding to this tension between adventure and security. Sociologists and informed churchmen might well be concerned for weightier reasons. The new congregations are prime examples of organizations forced to maintain a precarious balance between the energies devoted to their own security and the energies devoted to the accomplishment of their formal purposes. Numerous studies of educational, medical, political, religious, and governmental groups have shown how organizations under less trying circumstances can be diverted by secondary interests from the accomplishment of their expressed goals.[1]

There are two kinds of questions that follow from an interest in the development of new congregations. First, there is the descriptive question of how the character of the congregation compares with its formal goals. Such a query involves an understanding of the expressed goals of the congregation, the participants' understanding of these goals, and an assessment of how well the congregation's activities match its self-image. Second, there is the explanatory question of how the congregation comes to develop its character. An answer to this question must take into account the effects of pressures that are felt within any social group, and the social pressures that impinge upon the congregation from its environment. This description and explanation when combined provide a systematic picture which in spite of its weaknesses should enhance our understanding of new church development.

It was out of a combination of curiosity, religious concern, and academic interest about new church development that this book came to be written. In the pages that follow we will examine six new congregations in the light of the questions posed above. The perspective of the study should probably be called social-psychological. It is sociological in that it treats the congregation as a distinct operative unit; it is psychological in that it takes into account the attitudes of the persons who participate in the congregations. The implication of this approach which will be of greatest importance for most of the readers is that the congregation is treated herein as a social organization and not as a theological entity. As a result, there is no attempt to evaluate the character of the new congregations in terms of some transcendent criterion, or to suggest that they are "good" or "bad" in some ultimate sense.

The Six Congregations

Before beginning the study proper, the social subjects of this investigation should be introduced to the reader. The congregations are all Presbyterian and all are located near a metropolitan center on the Pacific Coast. Beyond that, they differ from each other in many respects, and taken together they probably represent most of the types of suburban congregations being established today. In the subsequent analysis the similarities in the development of the congregations will be emphasized with the necessary result that many of their idiosyncratic features will be dissolved. Therefore, it is fitting that they be presented here in their individuality.

The congregations were selected for the study specifically to include a variety of settings and experiences. Roughly, there were pairs of congregations in each of three categories of socioeconomic status determined from census data on income and education levels of the parish areas. Within each of the categories one of the congregations was selected because of a high rate of statistical growth in terms of membership and budget, and the other because of a relatively lower rate.

The Church of the Scattered. This congregation is located in an exclusive suburb where homes are well separated by hills and trees. Of the six areas, this one has the largest proportion of families earning over $10,000 per year (55 percent). It is situated about forty-five minutes from the city to which most of the men commute to work either in business or in one of the professions. Recently a number of housing tracts have been sprinkled through the area, providing a greater diversity in residents than was formerly true.

This congregation was the most statistically successful of the six. It was initiated by a group of laymen in the face of general pessimism on the part of the denominational agency. An energetic program of neighborhood meetings brought about a rapid growth of membership.

Subsequently, however, a split developed within the congregation that has crystallized into several factions. The church has been seeking ways of remedying the internal tension, but members reported a general decline in enthusiasm.

The Rustic Church. The parish area is in a wooded valley located well out of the way of the growing urban complex. Here one encounters signs along the narrow roadway that read: SLOW—EQUESTRIAN CROSSING, and at the modest shopping center, SILVERSMITH AND SADDLESMITH. The median family income is about $12,500 per year, and homes are valued at about $34,750. Nonresidential building has been kept to a minimum in the area, and the congregation had difficulty securing a Use Permit to erect a church building. Local people are much concerned with "society" life.

The congregation is small but relatively wealthy. It located when population growth was anticipated, but new construction has been slow. A nearby community church had resisted the establishment of a new congregation. Given the problem of finding land, the limited population, and the difficulties with the other church, this congregation has undergone a genuine test in getting settled.

The Parkside Church. This area has the highest education level of the six, with a median school years index of 15.0, and 42 percent of the male labor force in professional occupations. It is located in a new residential sector of one of the urban center's satellite cities. There is considerable commercial activity along the main routes bordering the area, but no nearby industry. The houses are

arranged in tracts, but they are reasonably expensive,
with the curving, rather than perpendicular, roadways
indicating that the builders had some interest in aesthe-
tics. The character of this congregation is described in
some detail in Chapter 8, "A 'Deviant' Case."

The Church on the Fringe. This congregation is located
on the very edge of the housing developments around
what was once a small town. The area is moderate on all
the indexes of status except for the proportion of professional workers, on which it is lowest (8.1 percent of the
male labor force). The men work at a variety of jobs,
both white- and blue-collar, as well as in small businesses.
There is a great diversity in the cost and nature of the
tracts that are served by the church, and perhaps for that
reason there is little sense of community in the area.

This congregation had perhaps the strongest start of
the six. Several large congregations contributed members
initially. However, the several backgrounds of the early
members became a basis for continuing divisions within
the congregation. The church's position on the outskirts
of the residential area has limited its subsequent growth
and the home-building that was anticipated has been curtailed by the purchase of nearby land by a private project.
However, the members are willing to commute some distance to support the congregation.

The Church of the Novices. Of the six, this area is lowest in family income ($7,504), median education, and
value of homes ($15,233). The occupations of the men
are various, with many lower white-collar jobs represented. The area is in a residential section of another
satellite city and offers quick commuting to work in not

too distant industrial areas. The homes are pleasant, but rather close together, and the pattern of the streets shows that the builders had an eye for economy. There is a rather high turnover of residents, many of whom seem to move on to other suburbs.

The congregation has a great diversity of backgrounds in its members. It began with few experienced leaders, but grew quickly with members learning by doing. The enthusiasm has been generally high. However, with the completion of the physical plant and the leveling of membership growth, a depression has set in. Most of the leaders feel the church has great potential, but is just now in a slump.

The Church on the Hillside. The parish area is relatively near to an industrial area and thus offers a convenience for commuters. The occupations of the residents are diverse. Houses are built close together but are attractively arranged along the contours of the hills. Sometimes the climate is cold, windy, and foggy. There seems to be a high rate of mobility in this area; some persons complain that they don't like the weather. Many of the residents are middle-aged; this area has the largest families of the six.

The congregation has suffered from two things. First, there has been a temporary curtailment of the housing development in which it is located, and this has limited the membership. Second, a controversy among the early members resulted in the departure of one group. As a result there has been difficulty in paying for the building. The congregation has one of the most imaginative programs of the six, but is constantly under pressure to find new members and to raise enough money to pay its bills.

These, then, are the congregations which have supplied the empirical data for this study. Each of them has its own distinctive characteristics. However, what is impressive is the extent to which they all have undergone very similar styles of development. It is because of this similarity in development that a study of six specific congregations can contribute to our general understanding of new church development.

The congregations described above are all part of The United Presbyterian Church U.S.A., and no special attention has been given below to the possible differences in development between these churches and those of other denominations. However, there are several reasons why the conclusions of this study may apply to the main-line Protestant groups generally. First, the differences in denominational activity are most visible in the structure of ecclesiastical government. At the congregational level there appears to be a minimal difference between denominations in what are considered to be appropriate activities. Second, the differences in doctrine of the main Protestant groups may be of less importance for the laity than for the clergy. Evidence to support this assumption can be found in the great amount of changing of denominations that is common in the mobile portion of our population. For these reasons the findings below may well apply across denominations.

The congregations with which we are concerned are all located in the suburbs of one metropolitan area in the West. Again, however, the relative similarity of suburban developments across the country, and the high mobility of the residents that gives them a common cosmopolitan tone, are reasons for seriously considering the relevance of such a study as this for churches in other areas. In itself the study of the church in the suburbs is a very timely one for both religion and sociology.

Finally, while this study concerns new churches, it may be of value to more established congregations. The specific forms by which pressures within and without are brought to bear on the congregation will differ for the two types of churches. But in many respects their similarity as social organizations will render conclusions about one of some relevance to the other. In short, this is not only a book about six congregations; to some extent all churches as social organizations are under analysis here.

2

THE CONGREGATION AS AN ORGANIZATION

It is not a primary interest of this book to develop a detailed theory of the congregation as a social organization. However, it is necessary to make explicit some assumptions in this regard in order to get on with the main topic. Although this study focuses on the new, suburban congregation, it uses as a tool of analysis a generalized conception of the Protestant congregation. Such a conceptualization has been given little attention by sociologists. Even though the local congregation is the main expression of the concrete organization of religious life in this country,[2] and normally exhibits such autonomy in its decisions that intervention from a higher bureaucracy is a rare and remarkable occurrence, it has been neglected in the bulk of religious research.

Since the contributions of Douglass and Brunner in the 1930's,[3] the work on religious organization in America has followed one of two directions. There have been, on the one hand, innumerable surveys dealing with the immediate environment of particular congregations with the purpose of helping them to evaluate their programs. Indeed, the work of Douglass and Brunner provided a strong impetus for this approach. However, this kind of effort, having a practical intent and a limited application, usually lacks a theoretical foundation and contributes little to our understanding of the congregation as an operating system.[4] This approach largely, if not wholly, consists of ecological and demographic descriptions of the parish and, while it can be valuable for specific cases, and indeed is necessary for subsequent explanatory work, it does not in itself further our understanding of the social dynamics of the congregation.

The second direction taken in the study of religious organization has been toward dealing with more complex units such as denominations,[5] or with church and sect differences,[6] or with religion as a general phenomenon and its place as an institution in social life.[7] Studies dealing with such large-scale phenomena allow for broad generalizations. However, it is a clear possibility that there are greater differences in religious attitudes and behavior between congregations of the same denomination than there are as a rule between denominations.[8] Further, it is not unlikely that the religious person is affected more by his experience in a particular congregation than he is by the characteristics of the tradition of which he is a member. The point here is that more consideration should be given to *types of congregations* as the most influential category of religious organization, and that theoretical conceptualization to this end is sorely needed.[9] This study suggests one approach to dealing with the congregation as an important religious force.

The Components of a Social Organization

Faced with a formal grouping of hundreds of persons and asked to explain something of why they behave as they do, the social scientist must necessarily make some decisions about how to divide this company into meaningful parts both to describe it and to discover its dynamics. His decisions are guided by the nature of his questions, by his personal inclinations, and by the work of other analysts who have dealt with a similar task. It is impossible to escape some portion of arbitrariness in this conceptualization of the phenomenon to be studied. As a result, it is necessary to spell out explicitly the rationale behind the approach that is employed in such a study as this.

A social organization is, in theoretical terms, a social system having formally defined boundaries. It can be recognized concretely as a group of persons distinguished from their social environment by a formally expressed purpose, formal definitions of membership, and recognized patterns of delegated authority. The congregation can be considered a social organization in these terms.

The root of this definition is "social system," a highly flexible concept that can be used to refer to any situation in which persons are interacting. The value of such a general concept is that it enables us to reason abstractly (rather than always specifically) about the conditions that are necessary for the existence of meaningful human cooperation. These reasonings can then be used for analytical purposes in the study of concrete social behavior. For this study, a variation of certain formulations of Talcott Parsons, which are presented in his general theory of social systems, will be utilized.[10]

Any social system, or social group, that persists for a significant period of time must deal in some manner with fundamental problems that arise whenever people attempt to cooperate with each other. One means of categorizing these "system problems" is to distinguish between those which have to do with the system's internal life, and those which are the result of the system's relation to its environment. These problems can also be distinguished as to whether they have to do with ends or with means to ends, that is, Are the problems related to matters that are consummatory or instrumental?

When these two distinctions are considered simultaneously, four areas of system problems are evident. (1) External-consummatory problems follow from efforts to realize the goals that society has come to expect from the system, or which the system professes. In the following analysis these problems will be spoken of as relating to the attainment of formal goals. (2) External-instrumental problems have to do with the adaptation of the system to its environment, which enables it to secure necessary resources and to defend itself from outside pressures. (3) Internal-consummatory problems have to do with the way participants are able to find satisfaction in being members of the system, and the kinds of incentive they have. (4) Internal-instrumental problems include those related to coordinating the activities within the system and maintaining its structure of relationships.

This scheme of "system problems" is an approximation of the functional requisites for social organizations proposed by Selznick and others.[11] For social organizations such as the congregation, we can specify the system problems as related to (1) attempts to specify and to realize formal goals, (2) the shaping of the program to adapt to the needs and demands of the environment, (3) the maintaining of morale of the members, and (4) the development of leaders and the maintaining of an authority structure. No claim is made that concrete reality is exactly analogous to the theoretical categories employed here. Rather, this scheme is adopted as a heuristic device to sensitize the investigator to relations between events, and makes possible a certain economy in organizing data.

The use of the approach outlined above for the study of organizations is of help also in avoiding a common difficulty. Amatai Etzioni suggested a few years ago that many organizational studies are inconsequential because they use a "goal model" in the study of institutional effectiveness.[12] In effect, this kind of analysis takes the formally stated goals as the only criterion for measuring efficiency. Etzioni maintains that there will invariably be a discrepancy between the ideal of the organization and the concrete entity because the means required to attain the formal goals are always greater than those available. This is a result of the fact that an organization is a composite of many diverse subunits and requires considerable effort simply to coordinate its parts. In other words, any organization has limited resources, some of which are required for functions not directly related to the attainment of its formal goals.

Consequently, although in this essay primary attention will be given to the congregation's efforts to realize its formal goals, due consideration will be given to the way these efforts are affected by the necessity of solving other problems of the organization. In terms of the conceptual framework employed here, the general question is, How does the congregation distribute its resources among the four system problems? Or, to narrow the focus, the question is, How does the amount of attention that is given to problems of morale, authority, and adaptation to the environment affect the congregation's attainment of its formal goals?

The Special Character of the Protestant Congregation

Not only have students of religion been negligent in investigating the nature of the congregation as an organization, the students of organizations have also shown little interest in the church. One reason for the silence of the latter may be that religious groups do not fit neatly into any of the popular typologies of organizations.[13] For whatever reasons, little has been said about the organizational type of religious organizations. The following description of the congregation is ordered according to the special conditions that relate to the four system problems.

Goal Attainment. What are the ends in terms of which the congregation rationalizes its existence? The congregation is dedicated to the service of God as he is described in its doctrine and experienced by its members. This service includes the honoring of the Deity and the nurture of individuals and the corporate life on the one hand, and the implementation of God's will in society on the other. The wide range of goals causes the congregation to overlap the categories of most typologies based on organizational purpose.[14] This wide range of goals is one of the distinctive characteristics of the congregation.

These goals, instead of being stated in specific terms, are cast in a very general mode. In part, this vagueness of statement is a result of the intention that local groups should interpret the goals in a manner most appropriate to the concrete situation in which they are located. In part, the goals are vague because they deal for the most part with qualities of human life and relationships that are difficult to measure in precise terms.

Finally, the congregation is in a unique position in that it receives support often for a secondary function—the statement of its intentions. That is, the congregation and the society see a value in the rehearsal of the goals of the congregation as a reminder of the ideals which the society is supposed to value, even if the congregation does not itself give striking, concrete service to the goals. Thus the congregation as an organization pursues goals which are wide-ranging, vaguely stated, and which are valued for their very expression.

Morale. What are the characteristics that distinguish the congregation in the integration of its participants? Perhaps more than any other organization, the congregation is open to everyone, provided they are willing to profess agreement with, and commitment to, its general goals. Glock has pointed out that the church is unique among voluntary associations in its commitment to serve both sexes and all ages. As a result, the membership of the congregation is likely to very heterogeneous, although usually limited by geographical location. Furthermore, the congregation is a voluntary association whose members are free to disassociate themselves at any time. If we overlook the fact that informal pressures from family, friends, and some communities incline persons to participation, it is clear that the congregation has a formidable task to maintain their allegiance. This task is more difficult than in other voluntary organizations because the congregation asks the member to commit himself to service in his whole life rather than as an extracurricular activity. Quite possibly only radical political organizations and such quasi-religious groups as Alcoholics Anonymous have this same characteristic or an approximation of it. Moreover, the congregation asks for service that involves the sacrifice of some self-interest.

One of the levers that the congregation has to maintain membership loyalty is the appeal to the legitimacy of its activity. This legitimacy rests on the acceptance by the member of a supernatural or superhistorical authority whose agent is the congregation. It is quite possible that this kind of legitimacy is increasingly imperiled as society turns from the authority of "tradition" to the authority of "reason." The other main lever by which the congregation maintains loyalty is to serve some interest of the member. The danger in maintaining integration through special interests is that the loyalty of the members is only momentary, and even while they are participating they may be only segmentally involved, with little concern for the overall purpose of the congregation. Actually, the congregation is likely to have a mixture of reasons among the members for participation at any moment.

Authority. Where is the authority by which the patterns of behavior in the congregation are coordinated and ordered? The ultimate source of authority is in the acceptance of supernatural or superhistorical authority that was mentioned above. Where this acceptance is not present, the task of implementing goals beyond certain limited interests is very difficult. The task in the congregation falls to its professional staff member, the minister. He is paid both to serve and to lead the congregation, and the difficulties which follow from these opposite demands have been noted in several sociological papers.[15] To complicate further his role, the minister is responsible to a board of laymen elected by his congregation, and to a regional assembly of ministers and lay leaders. Within this web of diverse authorities, the minister must both teach and implement the goals of the congregation, and oversee the practical problems that accompany the operation of an organization. Through a number of channels the minister is also heir to recommendations from the national bureaucracy.

The largest part of the decisions concerning the congregation are made by the minister and the lay leaders. Since these leaders are democratically elected, there is the constant danger that they will be selected for reasons which are rather peripheral to the main goals of the congregation. This is especially true where practical concerns are very evident and there are specialists present who are particularly competent to deal with them. The offices that the leaders fill usually have responsibilities broad enough that specialists can come into positions which involve them in religious leadership for which they have little capacity or inclination. The minister, whose training is in religious matters, does not have a very free hand.

Adaptation. The congregation is a private organization but is not run for profit, and is dependent upon the voluntary support of the community around it. It is supposed to be both prophet and servant to the people it contacts. Thus, to some extent it must meet their expectations and to some extent change them. It is a precarious balance to maintain.

On the one hand, the congregation is in the business of maintaining a tradition with its peculiar symbols. Its actual and potential members expect certain fundamental things from it in the way of building, program, and polity. On the other hand, the congregation may try to alter an aspect of the social environment in the course of which effort it runs the risk of alienating some persons. Since the congregation depends upon these persons for its resources, it may have to compromise some of its goals in order to attain others. It is the locating of the optimum balance in this regard that is the dilemma of the modern church.

Nor does the congregation have a specific clientele that it serves. It must decide on the basis of the concrete conditions how far it will range into the community in its activities. In its work it must also consider the sentiments of other congregations if it is to avoid debilitating conflict or competition.

The New Suburban Congregation

The chief concern of this study is with the characteristics of the new suburban congregation, and it will be helpful at this point to note some of the conditions that are peculiar to it. Suburb is defined as those recent developments (usually tracts) which are almost exclusively given to housing units constructed in groups and located near an urban area. This definition is intended to exclude random houses in what is called the urban-rural fringe and which may have their own distinctive characteristics. There have been a number of books recently which give diverse pictures of this area.[16]

The Suburban Context. Whatever may be the overall picture of suburban developments in this country, the areas in this study, though they ranged from working-class to upper-middle-class, were relatively homogeneous. This is not surprising, since the homes built within an area by one contractor tend to be in a narrow price range.

Thus the area that a suburban congregation serves is likely to contain persons in similar kinds of circumstances. In this characteristic, the suburban congregation differs from its small-town counterpart, and to some extent from its urban counterpart.

The homogeneity of its clientele has implications for the programming of the congregation. In particular, the members are likely to be at nearly the same stage in the life cycle, so that parents of a particular age and children of a particular age become the chief concern. There are few older persons, and few in the twenty-year gap between parents and children.

The homogeneity might seem to be of great benefit in combining the congregations into close fellowships, since incomes are relatively the same, families are nearly the same, and the problems of both are shared. But the suburbs also have a high rate of transiency. Persons who gain advancement, which the suburbanites are likely to do since they are in the prime of life, tend to move to a more highly priced suburb. Many of the persons in the income bracket that allows for suburban living are also committed either to move when their companies desire it or to sacrifice their jobs. This transiency is not likely to affect the new congregation for several years, but just as it is rounding into good form there is likely to be a departure of some of the key personnel. All the congregations reported this as a difficulty.

Although the congregations may be homogeneous in some respects, they certainly are not with regard to religious backgrounds. Brought together by the proximity of their jobs to the suburb, or by housing congenial to their income, suburbanites are drawn from the whole range of denominations. Many of them have had no background

in any church. Of those who have been in churches,
there are not many of the younger people who had been
very active. The upper-middle-class suburbs which have
somewhat older residents are likely to have more persons
who have been active in the church. At any rate, the
suburban congregation has the one big task of welding
together members from a diversity of backgrounds.

Regardless of religious experience, leadership potential
seems to vary with the status of the suburb. Those congregations in the working-class areas felt hard pressed to
find lay leaders. The congregations at the other end of
the status scale had a problem with too many of the
members being eager to take on some kind of authority
position. The congregations have been forced to train all
of their leaders on the one hand, and to spend considerable time in coordinating organization on the other. Those
in the middle-class suburbs did not have this kind of difficulty. A problem that is implicit in a surfeit of potential
leaders is that persons with practical abilities will attain
positions of responsibility without having essential religious understanding or commitments.

Because of the newness of the area in which it is located, the suburban congregation finds itself in a community without a center. Houses, schools, and shopping
centers stand where there were none before. There are
few if any local papers. There is nothing that distinguishes the area except the name which it bears. There
are few, if any, of the activities that go with commercial,
industrial, or entertainment centers. In this situation, it is
understandable that people would look for some kind of
focus, a source of identity, something familiar, a continuity with past life, a place for roots. Eventually there
will be informal groupings, and the spread of commercial

enterprises, but for the early residents there is little beside the church, the shopping center, and perhaps a
home owners association to bring the neighborhood together. At this point the congregation seriously faces the
dilemma of how far it can go in serving as a community
center without losing completely the uniqueness of its
mission or goals. Because of its position in the new community, it is likely to gather a great many segmental, and
therefore temporary, participants.

Furthermore, the suburbs are relatively affluent. There
is little or no poverty, disease, or crime; there are likely
to be few if any members of racial minorities; the physical plants are too new to show much deterioration; the
residents are in the prime of life. Aside from such pri-
vatized family troubles as juvenile lawlessness or marital
difficulties, there is not much that could be termed social
problems in the community. The congregation in this
situation may have to look hard for an outlet for such
intentions of service as it might have. To attack such
ethical problems as closed or restricted housing practices
requires considerable courage, and there is a distinct
danger that the new congregation will be satisfied to
internalize its activities.

The New Congregation. The new congregation is described not in terms of what it is, but in terms of what it
is not. The two most significant lacks are those of a continuing personnel and of a formalized or traditional program. Its personnel are not acquainted with each other for
the most part, which makes for initial difficulties in communication. The lack of formalized procedures means not
only that the possibilities for the future are many, but
also that there are few guidelines to facilitate coopera-

tion. Because of the lack of leadership, persons must be pressed into service before anyone has a clear idea of their competence or potential. To overcome these difficulties, there is a need for a considerable amount of blind trust on the part of the members of the new congregation: trust of the minister and of each other.

This necessary trust, along with the adventure of starting a somewhat risky venture, usually eventuates in considerable enthusiasm in the early stages. Directing the enthusiasm can be a difficult job, and an important one, for the shape of the established congregation is to a large extent determined in the early stages. It is the main task of this study to explore just how the new congregation gets started, and how its initial direction affects its later character.

In this study, the congregation's life has been divided into two stages—the "developing" congregation and the "developed" congregation. The developing congregation is characterized by the statements above about the new congregation. The developed congregation refers to the state after the work of establishment has been completed: the congregation when it is considered to be "here to stay."

There is no single, clear watershed that marks the boundary between these two stages of the congregation's life, but the division is roughly indicated by the coincidence of several events: the leveling off of membership growth, the completion of most of the physical plant, and the attainment of a rather consistent financial support. Although these events do not necessarily occur at the same time, and although their order varies with the conditions of the particular congregation, they generally are accumulated within a relatively short time span. Our interest is in the periods on either side of this time span, the first characterized by a desire for permanence, and the second by an assumption of permanence.

Because the attitudes and conditions of the congregations at these two periods differ, they will be treated separately. For each period, we will examine the character of the congregation in relation to its formal goals, and the factors that seem to shape their character. Chapters 4 and 5 will deal with the developing congregation, and Chapters 6 and 7 with the developed congregation.

3

THE GOALS OF THE CONGREGATION

Our main interest in this book is in the manner in which the conditions of the new congregation affect its efforts at goal attainment. The criterion or standpoint from which these efforts must in part be evaluated is that of the congregation's formal goals. There are two processes intermingled in the congregation's efforts: one has to do with the definition of goals, and the other has to do with concrete activity related to the definitions. In the present chapter, the chief concern is with definitions of the goals.

The formal goals of the congregation are in reality the goals of the church (theologically defined), of which the congregation is the proximate empirical expression. These goals are derived from the Scriptures and other writings of which the tradition of the church is composed, are stated in explicit, though general, terms in the official documents of the denominational organization, and are interpreted and applied through the elaborations of theologians, ministers, and church members. Thus, for such an analysis as is undertaken here there must be a translation of the general goals of the church into the activities of the congregation. And since the goals are stated in theological language, they must be translated into socio-logical language. The dual translation is the purpose of this chapter.

The sources of data for such a translation are two. First, we will refer to the writings of theological com-mentators whose popularity both with religious leaders and with lay members, together with their professional standing, places them in conspicuous positions as spokes-men for the church in contemporary America. From these sources we will gain some general understanding of the church as a social entity. Second, we will refer to de-nominational documents that give official sanctions to these goals. Taken together, the two sources will provide a basis for constructing a picture of the formal goals that are applicable to the congregation.

It should be made clear at this point that there is tre-mendous variation in the interpretation of the goals (mis-sion, purpose, aim, end) of the church. The constant debate that goes on within the church, the divisions that reflect differing views, the difficulty of broad cooperation between groups, all point to the fact that there has been no final, authoritative determination of substantive goals. As a result, any formulation can be accused of being arbi-trary, and that is certainly true of the statements made here. The fact that the goals presented in this paper are repeatedly mentioned by persons concerned with the re-vitalization of the church lends some support to their validity. Further, these statements of goals are very much in line with the positions taken by the ministers who participated in the study, and have been characteristic of material from the national agencies of the United Pres-byterian Church. The value of the subsequent analysis in this paper necessarily rests upon the accuracy of its assessment of the formal goals.

Themes in Contemporary Theology

The outstanding feature of the church's expressions of its goals is their generality and vagueness. This feature together with its consequences are treated in some detail in a paper by Glock.[17] To illustrate the point, it is only necessary to refer to the work of one of the leading theologians of the contemporary scene who was also a sometime sociologist, the late H. Richard Niebuhr. In a paper bearing directly on the topic of concern here, Niebuhr wrote:

> There is no single norm of the Christian religion which enables an observer to say that the religious institution which possesses the character described is "really" Christian. . . . Its norm is the concrete mind of Christ and therefore the faith and the hope and the desire of Christ.[18]

Later, in connection with a sociological study of theological education, he wrote:

> No substitute can be found for the definition of the goal of the Church as the *increase among men of the love of God and neighbor.*[19]

Although this mode of vagueness deals with the form rather than the substance of the church's goals, it is necessary to make it explicit here because it will have bearing on the congregation's attempts to give empirical content to the goals.

There are four important and recurring themes in contemporary theology which are related to the church's goals and which can be related to the final objectives of the congregation. One is related to the quality of internal life of the congregation; a second deals with the intentions of the congregation with regard to the individual;

and the third is concerned with the congregation's responsibility for the society around it. The fourth theme, which is of particular interest from a sociological standpoint, has to do with the manner in which the congregation assigns priorities to its goals.

The Congregation as Community. One of the leading themes in modern theology is that of the congregation as community. It emphasizes the importance of the quality of personal relationships in contrast to the formal associations that result from mere participation in a structured organization. The writing about this quality of community in the congregation has gone back to a New Testament term for the church, *koinōnia,* as a concept of the ideal. Martin Marty, one of the most well-known and widely read clergymen in the United States today, puts it this way:

> Ecclesiology and anthropology have been fused in the study of the New Testament description of the *koinonia,* the shared life. Here the horizontal relations of man to men are characterized by participation in the divine life which is a gift from Christ (a vertical relationship). Here there grows a partnership of loving service and unity which draws its strength from the remembrance of Jesus Christ and the contemporaneity of his gifts.[20]

The main points of this statement are the common relation to the Deity and the quality of the relationships between members. Put in other terms, they mean that the congregation will center its corporate life around the worship of God, and in this unity will achieve a community of trust and honesty encouraged by the sharing of ultimate convictions. This community offers the members encouragement for their individual efforts, and support in their difficulties. It exists where there is a lack of divisiveness about beliefs, and where there is a network of deep friendships.

Marty is careful to distinguish this koinonia relationship from the "togetherness" theme which has been so popular in recent years. The Christian community does not call for the individual to lose himself in the group, but rather for a double emphasis on human freedom and relationships of trust and honesty.

This community is Peter Berger's interest too (although he disagrees with Marty as to how it can be realized) when he suggests that perhaps the organizational forms of Christianity as they now exist must be abandoned by some, or many, in an effort to find again the true fellowship.[21] His dispute with the neo-orthodox postulation of the koinonia is not about the nature or desirability of it, but at the seeming impossibility of establishing it within the present organizational structures. He fears that the operations of the congregations have become so routinized that personal relationships are very difficult to establish.

The marks of the community aspect of the congregation are a sense of unity of purpose, patience in dealing with differences, and an atmosphere that encourages close personal ties. Its absence is indicated by a lack of clear purpose, the formation of factions, and a general lack of close relationships with the congregation. In the large congregations that are becoming the norm today, it is likely that where such community is present it will be in subgroups within the congregation rather than encompassing the entire membership. Where such small communities exist, however, it would seem that they would be open to new participants, and base their mem-

bership (however informal it might be) on evidence of
commitment rather than on characteristics less germane
to the overall life of the congregation.

The Congregation as a Place for Nurture. There have
been a great many books recently that deal with the cen-
trality of the layman in the work of the church.[22] They
stress the fact that it is the individual Christian who
represents the church and not the professional clergy.
And they lament the fact that too often the ministers are
seen as the representatives of the members in carrying
out the mission of the church in the world as trained
substitutes for them. The Bishop of Woolwich expresses
it this way:

> It is essential that we do see it this way round—that the
> clergy are the servants of the laity. As Hans-Ruedi Weber
> has put it: "The laity are not helpers of the clergy so
> that the clergy can do their job, but the clergy are
> helpers of the whole people of God, so that the laity can
> be the Church."[23]

Gibson Winter speaks of the organization church, hope-
fully, as a "co-ordination of the ministries of members."[24]
And the same theme is present in Peter L. Berger's call
for a strengthening of a "Christian diaconate," and for a
closer conversation between the Christian faith and the
everyday vocations of Christians.[25]

It is not only the members' reliance upon the ministers
that is called into question here, but also the reliance on
the bureaucracy of the larger organized church to express, to carry out, the work of the whole church. It is a
criticism of the tendency for members to feel that by
financing the organization they are fulfilling any obligations they may have to the God they profess to worship.

The implications of this theme for the congregation are that the congregation must provide for the proper education of its members, and must encourage the acceptance of responsibility on their part. This responsibility is to be exercised in their whole lives, which means in the leadership of the congregation and in the furthering of the church's mission in society. It means that study should be fostered, that authority should be shared, and that there should be the kind of communication that makes known the ways and means by which members are uniquely serving the church in their daily rounds.

Where the congregation is not carrying out its activities properly in the nurture of its members, there is likely to be a lack of significant adult education along with weak church school programs (dependent as they are upon the training of the adults as teachers), a limited turnover of lay officials, and considerable pride in the amount of the church funds going to benevolences and the amount of time put into congregational activities. In capsule form, the picture is one of limited growth by the members either in depth or in breadth.

The Congregation as Servant. One of the characteristics of the church is that it intends to be not only consummatory, but also instrumental. Part of its instrumental function is expressed in the nurture of its members; another part is seen in its efforts to alter the character of social life in the world. It is not dedicated to the maintenance of the present social order, but to the expression of certain values in the concrete life of everyday. Both as a corporate entity and through the ministrations of its individual members it directs its attention to the "secular" world to which (in theological terms) it has

been sent. In a reference to the important work of
Hendrik Kraemer, Gibson Winter expresses this theme:

> There is much talk in theological circles about the
> "Church as Mission" and the "Church's Mission"; theo-
> logians have been stressing the fact that the Church
> does not exist for its own sake but as a testimony in
> the world for the healing of the world. . . . To be the
> Church is to *participate* in the world to which the
> Church is sent.[26]

The claim that the church's primary consideration is not
its own life but the service to the whole world for which
it was established is reiterated by Niebuhr and Marty.

> Whether the term Church or the term Christianity is
> used, there is an internal contradiction in a theology
> and a Christian educational system that regard the work
> of the Church as the final activity to be considered.[27]

> The creative local church carries on its mission to the
> community for the community's sake. It serves for in-
> trinsic reasons. Its actions are more often pre-evangeli-
> cal. As time passes, opportunities will usually grow for
> overt evangelism, verbal contact. This sequence—begin-
> ning with intrinsic service, following with pre-evangeli-
> cal contact, and only then making the verbal approach
> —reverses the right sequence in the eyes of many. Does
> it amount to "being ashamed of the offense of the
> Gospel"? No; rather, with ingenuity, it seeks to locate
> the actual offense of the Gospel in the new setting. It
> provides a sound approach to the real centers of the
> community and not just to the religiously precondi-
> tioned, the nice safe people who want the church to
> remove them from responsibility.[28]

The same theme is given a somewhat more official status
by the United Presbyterian Church's Standing Committee on Social Education and Action, reporting in 1955.

Churches and individual Christians who seek to "glorify God" *only* through hymns and prayers and "living a good life" are sinning against their God.[29]

One condition needs to be placed on what has just been said: the church intends to serve the needs of the world, but reserves the right to define what the real needs are. That is, it determines to enter into conversation about the problems of the age, but it does not become a baby-sitter just because someone feels he needs a baby-sitter.

For the congregation as an organization, this theme in the church's formal goals means that the activity of the congregation should be directed to some service beyond its own inner life. The main task is found in the congregation's contact with its environment. The task consists in the promotion of the ethics of the Christian tradition in social relations: the promotion of justice, reconciliation of conflicts, and the relief of suffering. Perhaps no clearer exercise in behalf of this goal can be found than the recent involvement of the churches in the civil rights movement, not only in protests at far-off racial inequities, but in attempts to improve conditions in their immediate neighborhoods.

The danger that the congregation will misinterpret the goals of service looms largest in those areas which are concerned with its own well-being. The congregation that conceives of service through recruitment to its own membership, or through its contributions to the denominational hierarchy, has missed the point. The congregation that conceives of service as the functions it carries out for its own members is mistaken in the same way. Perhaps the key distinction between service and these activities is the "intrinsic" nature of the former, as Marty puts it. Service is valuable in itself and apart from any explicitly religious associations.

The Congregation as Sacrificial. This final theme of
contemporary theology has to do with the standard by
which the congregation assigns priorities to its goals. As
such, it is of central importance to the topic of this study.
And it is of particular sociological interest in the way it
reduces to a secondary status efforts for organizational
survival.

This theme of the church as sacrificial which has been
widely treated in contemporary theology essentially af-
firms the "Protestant principle" as it has been defined by
Paul Tillich.[30] Tillich sees the unique emphasis of Protestantism as being that no concrete form, whether object
or thought, can be accorded divine status free from criticism. The organizational forms that the church has
adopted are also heir to criticism from this point of view.
The question is being more and more frequently raised
as to how the church should shape itself in order to meet
adequately the varying needs of the rural, suburban, and
inner-city contexts in which it works.

In this regard there is an emphasis on the congregation's being willing to sacrifice its form in order to realize
its primary goals. The theological assumption that under-
lies this emphasis is that the church as God's instrument
will not perish even if its present concrete expressions do.
The commentaries on this theme range from suggestions
that there be a wholesale abandonment of the organized
church[31] to attempts at new approaches supported by
traditional means.[32] Martin Marty illustrates these expressions in pointing to a series on "Creative Churches in
America" run by *The Christian Century.*

> The editors were in quest of churches which were biting
> off problems larger than they could reasonably expect
> to manage and were ready to risk failure in the attempt.[33]

An example of just such a church which continually pushes out into forms of expression that outrage "good business sense" is the Church of the Savior in Washington, D.C.[34] On numerous occasions, such as the establishment of its coffeehouse, retreat center, and workshops, the church has felt "called" to implement programs for which it had few apparent resources at the outset. Its record of faithful but risky service is again and again cited as an illustration of the ideal by Protestants.

The importance of this theme for the congregation as an organization is that survival in itself should not be taken as a primary goal. In fact, the congregation should be sufficiently dedicated to its formal goals that it is willing to risk not surviving as an organized unit. A dramatic but appropriate analogy would be the commando unit that enters each mission with the understanding that the dedication to the accomplishment of the objective outweighs any considerations for its own survival. In the same way, the congregation weighs its decisions in terms of their value for realizing its primary objectives. In practical terms, this means that catering to the wishes of prominent members, shaping programs with an eye to financial returns, and keeping to a middle ground that will not antagonize anyone is an abandonment of the congregation's sacrificial character. The proper alternative is to decide on the best expression of the congregation's goals first and then to let the chips fall where they may.

These themes which dominate contemporary theological writing on the organized church are rooted in traditional expressions of the church's goals. But the themes do more than indicate the direction of the thinking of some church leaders; they also provide a context for the interpretation of the traditional expressions. They set a tone that can be used to organize and summarize official doctrines.

Goals in the Official Documents

Each person who desires to become a formal member of a congregation of the United Presbyterian Church is asked to assent to three statements (after his request has been approved by the ruling board of the congregation). The exact wording of these statements follows:

(1) Do you confess your faith in God the Father Almighty, Maker of heaven and earth, and in Jesus Christ his only Son our Lord, and do you promise with the aid of the Holy Spirit to be Christ's faithful disciple to your life's end?

(2) Do you confirm the vows taken for you in Baptism, and with a humble and contrite heart put your whole trust in the mercy of God which is in Christ our Lord?

(3) Do you promise to make diligent use of the means of grace, to share faithfully in the worship and service of the Church, to give of your substance as the Lord may prosper you, to give your whole heart to the service of Christ and his Kingdom throughout the world, and to continue in the peace and fellowship of the people of God?[35]

The generality of the vow is evident. The individual is asked to affirm his condition of faith, his intention to participate in religious observances, his willingness to be of service both inside and outside the church, and to share his worldly means. The concrete interpretation of these statements is left up to the individual and, by implication, to the congregation of which he is a member. To approach more closely an idea of what might be expected

of the church member, we can turn to the statements
approved by the denomination about the activities of the
local congregation.

The great ends of the Church are the proclamation of
the gospel for the salvation of men; the shelter, nurture,
and spiritual fellowship of the children of God; the
maintenance of divine worship; the preservation of the
truth; the promotion of social righteousness; and the exhibition of the Kingdom of Heaven to the world. (Ch.
III, Sec. 4.)

Communions and particular churches ought to co-oper-
ate in so far as possible in giving expression to their
oneness in Jesus Christ within his body, the ecumenical,
catholic Church. (Ch. III, Sec. 5.)

A particular church consists of a number of professing
Christians, with their children, voluntarily associated
together for divine worship and godly living, agreeably
to the Holy Scriptures, and submitting to a certain form
of government. (Ch. IV, Sec. 1.)

The ordinances established by Christ, the head, in a
particular church are prayer, singing praises, reading,
expounding and preaching the Word of God; administering Baptism and the Lord's Supper; thanksgiving,
catechizing, making collections for the poor and other
pious purposes; exercising discipline; and blessing the
people. (Ch. IV, Sec. 3.)

Church members are under obligation to make diligent
use of the means of grace, to share faithfully in the
worship and service of the Church, to give of their substance as the Lord may prosper them, to render wholehearted service to Christ and his Kingdom throughout
the world, and to continue in the peace and fellowship
of the people of God. (Ch. VI, Sec. 3.)[36]

These statements can be taken as an outline of the authoritative normative objectives of the church, and thus of the particular congregations that are its parts. For analytic purposes, these statements can be summarized according to the nature of the activity implicit in them. In keeping the general themes noted above, the intentions of the congregation can be expressed in terms of a number of topically related goals.

First, the church directs part of its effort to establishing a particular kind of internal association around its beliefs and the ritual that rehearses them: "the maintenance of divine worship . . . prayer, singing praises . . . thanksgiving . . . administering Baptism and the Lord's Supper." Another aspect is the government and ordering of the congregational life. And a third has to do with the quality of personal relations within the congregation: "spiritual fellowship of the children of God . . . giving expression to their oneness in Jesus Christ within his body . . . to continue in the peace and fellowship of the people of God." Thus efforts are directed to shaping the congregation into a disciplined fellowship centering around worship.

Second, there is the interest of the church in spreading its influence through the efforts of individual members in their various stations in daily life. To this end, the church minimizes the professionalization of its ministry and promotes instead the understanding that all believers, ministers and laymen, serve equally. It supports programs that lead to the nurture of members through education, solicits their leadership in the government of the church itself, and encourages their expressing their convictions in the world around them. Two emphases are important here: the explicit identification of the layman as an individual agent over against the congregation as a corporate agent, and the service of the layman in his daily life rather than only in the congregation. The education and nurturing functions of the congregation are expressed as: "living, agreeably to the Holy Scriptures . . . catechizing . . . reading, expounding and preaching the Word of God . . . the preservation of the truth." The members are encouraged as individuals to: "give of their substance as the Lord may prosper them . . . to render wholehearted service to Christ and his Kingdom throughout the world."

Third, there are the concrete acts by which the congregation as a corporate entity approaches the world around it. These acts can be considered as explicitly religious or implicitly religious. The former category includes "the proclamation of the gospel" and those activities which call for a decision on the part of the uncommitted about the church and its beliefs. The latter category includes attempts to alter the secular world according to the pattern of the church's idea of society. This is expressed in: "collections for the poor . . . the exhibition of the Kingdom of Heaven to the world . . . the promotion of social righteousness." Together we can describe these objectives as the service of the church in the world.

Within each of the three topical categories, there are several emphases which are not to be taken as alternatives, but rather as *multiple imperatives* for the congregation. Each of these emphases can be linked with concrete activities (although a number of activities could be taken as the expression of any emphasis), so that the absence of relevant activities indicates an absence of expression of that particular emphasis. In the following section these emphases will be spelled out as the formal goals of the congregation.

Multiple Imperatives: The Formal Goals of the Congregation

The formal goals of the congregation are the explicitly stated objectives that the organization intends to use as criteria for evaluating its activities. In a sense, they describe the "ideal" congregation. By collating the theological themes in contemporary writing with the official statements of the United Presbyterian Church, one can arrive at a formulation of the formal goals of the congregation which has reasonable claim to validity. While it would be extremely difficult to decide between alternative formulations on such a concrete level, at least the one adopted here cannot be rejected out of hand.

Community. One of the goals of the congregation is to establish a sense of community among its members which centers around shared beliefs and the ritual rehearsals of them, is ordered according to a formal discipline, and evidences a quality of trust and honesty that supports and comforts the members. There are three characteristics that mark the realization of this goal. First, there is a unity of belief, or at least sufficient unity so that variations are tolerated, and widespread support of the congregation's services of worship. Second, there is an acceptance of the form of government that is practiced and of those in positions of authority, and a general participation in the offices and meetings of the congregation. Third, there is a fellowship among the members of a quality that encourages candor and fosters a feeling of security. The congregation has an "at home" atmosphere where matters of such importance are shared that close personal ties are formed and retained.

Where the goal of community is not attained, it will be apparent in a number of ways. There may be dissatisfaction with the leadership of the congregation: a feeling that either the personnel are not competent or that their views are faulty. In extreme cases this dissatisfaction may be directed at the minister himself. There may be factions within the congregation that have developed because of differences in doctrinal understandings—factions which form around any number of specifics, and which lead to crises in the congregational life. These crises show not so much the presence of differences as the lack of an attitude of tolerance that is essential for resolving them. Finally, there may be a lack of close personal relationships within the congregation, a sign that the congregation has not got beyond its formal structures to the fellowship atmosphere that it desires.

Nurture. By nurture we refer to a second goal of the congregation, the intention to equip each member to carry out his unique expression of the congregation's mission. The overriding aim is to encourage in the individual the understanding that all believers are equal in their service and that there is no organizational machinery that can validly be considered a substitute in carrying out the member's responsibility. The several characteristics that mark the realization of this goal are: a program of continuing education that includes all members, a continual and widespread changing and sharing of the authority positions within the congregation, and some means for communicating the intentional activities of the members in their extracongregational efforts to further the church's aims in the secular world.

The failure to attain this goal is most likely to be seen

in one of the following ways: The educational program
is for the most part limited to work with children in the
church school program. Laymen are excluded from participation in the leadership of the worship services of the
congregation. The lay leadership of the congregation becomes entrenched in its positions so that the same members
are repeatedly elected to the same offices (allowing for
the minimum rotation that will meet formal requirements). There are no means within the program of the
congregation by which members can share what they as
individuals are attempting to do to further the congregation's mission in their daily lives. The mission of the
church is generally expressed in terms of the efforts of the
professional clergy, or in terms of the work of the wider
organization to which the congregation makes financial
contributions. In any or all of these ways the congregation can evidence a lack of nurture of its members.

Service. Finally, the congregation intends to serve its
God as a corporate body. It does this either by explicitly
confronting the world with its beliefs and asking for a
direct response, or by working to alter the social relations
of men to be more in accord with its religious precepts.
The explicitly religious efforts are spoken of under the
term "evangelism." The congregation that attempts to
realize the goal of service will do so in part by making
known its religious position to persons who come to its
attention, such as new residents in the community. The
congregation also serves in an implicitly religious manner
by working for the improvement of society through the
reconciliation of conflicting factions, the furthering of
justice, and the relief of suffering. Both of these approaches should be exercised where the congregation
properly pursues its goal of service.

Where this goal is not realized, the congregation is, at an extreme, likely to internalize its attention. It becomes a closed group and ignores the world around it. In a less extreme form it may become an agent of only the explicitly religious aspects of its service, the fruits of its efforts being largely the recruitment of new members. The congregation's failure in this regard will be evident in a lack of any significant wrestling with the real social conditions of the world outside its walls.

The Relation of Formal Goals and Survival Goals

For the purposes of this essay, "survival goals" are those ends which the participants feel must be sought if the congregation is to continue *as an organization*. They involve operations that apparently must be carried out if the social structure of the congregation is not to dissolve. In specific terms, the survival goals are the recruiting and maintaining of members, the establishment of physical facilities, and the stabilization of a base of financial support. The term "goals" has been attached to these tasks because they can become in a real sense the primary focus of attention for the members to the exclusion of the formal goals. They are not simply means to formal ends, but become ends in themselves.[37]

The concept of survival goals should not be confused with survival in the more restricted sense of maintaining institutional integrity. Where this use of "survival" refers to the continuation of the organization *with* a persisting active dedication to its formal goals, "survival goals" are concerned with the continuation of the organization without reference to its service to the formal goals.

Survival goals also differ from the sociologically analytical idea of survival which describes activities in terms of their functions for the maintenance of the system. In this sense, certain activities are defined by observers as functional requisites for the survival of the organization.[38] Survival goals, on the other hand, are the tasks that *participants* see as essential for the organization, rather than what the analyst defines as essential.

Formal goals and survival goals are not necessarily in conflict. The former imply the latter. That is, if the formal goals are to be realized, then the survival goals must be accomplished in some fashion. When, however, the congregation becomes oriented around survival goals to such an extent that it neglects the formal goals, we can talk about a conflict between them. It is a special kind of conflict in which the elevation of secondary concerns brings about an eclipse of primary concerns. Instead of the pursuit of the formal goals forcing the participants to pay some attention to the survival goals, the survival goals are sought first while the formal goals are deferred.

Survival goals can be rationalized in terms of the formal goals. The recruitment of members can be called evangelism; the financing of the program and the construction of buildings, stewardship; the maintenance of members through social programs, fellowship. However, the activities related to the survival goals do not exhaust the intentions of the formal goals. The important question is that of whether the congregation puts any effort into these aspects of the formal goals which do not directly contribute to the survival goals. Where the congregation attempts to realize its formal goals only in ways which can also be seen as serving survival goals, it can be suggested that the survival goals have become primary to the congregation. It is precisely this possibility which is examined below.

4

CONFLICT IN THE DEVELOPING CONGREGATION

It is understandable that persons affiliate with voluntary groups for any number of personal reasons that have little to do with the formal ends of the groups. It is perhaps less common that the members of an association are in doubt about what its goals are. Yet this is precisely the case with the congregation. The vagueness with which the formal goals of the congregation are stated attracts to it members of great diversity and opens it to misunderstanding, confusion, and conflict.[39] The vagueness of the goals does not in itself make conflict inevitable, but it is a condition from which conflict can easily develop. Because the formal goals must be translated into concrete terms if specific activities are to be directed to the realization of the goals, it becomes necessary to arrive at some agreement about the translation. In the developing congregation the members have gathered around the vaguely stated formal goals rather than around some concrete expression of them. Since they come from a variety of backgrounds, they bring a variety of understandings about how the goals should be translated. It is this diversity, together with the vague goals, that leads to conflict.

In this chapter we shall treat the nature of goal conflict in the developing congregation, and some of its causes.

In the following chapter we will give an account of the pressures that make for the particular resolution in terms of survival goals, and a description of the character of the congregation that results.

The Nature of the Conflict: Multiple Viewpoints

We can distinguish two kinds of conflict in the developing congregation defined in terms of the contending parties. First, there is a conflict of understanding between the minister and most of the members. Second, there is a conflict of intention between various groups of the members.

The Ministers' Perceptions of the Goals. The ministers generally state their conceptions of the congregation's formal goals in theological, or at least abstract, terms. This is probably due in part to the fact that they have studied these matters more fully and have arrived at certain forms of expression which are particularly meaningful to them. The fact that they are dealing with a group of persons who, if the formal goals are to be expressed in their daily lives, must adapt them to different concrete situations, is probably another reason for stating the goals in broad terms.

The ministers stated that their intentions at the outset were to establish "a community of worship, nurture, and mission." While their particular expressions differed, they all viewed the goals of the congregation as centering in these themes. Their early efforts were largely directed to creating an understanding of this kind within the membership.

"Mission was uppermost in our minds. We wanted to develop a worshiping community that was learning and serving. We wanted the congregation to be alive."

"We wanted to get believers together, establish a sense of the church as the unit of life that gives it away, and find our mission."

"Our unique task was the communication of the gospel in the largest sense of the term to the community situation. What this implied for this congregation was the destruction of false stereotypes about the church, and the realization of community in terms of a redemptive fellowship that was open and accepting."

None of the ministers mentioned the construction of a physical plant or the raising of funds as a particular consideration at the beginning. Only one of the men felt that the recruitment of members was accorded a prime place in his early intentions. While these survival-goal concerns may have been implicit in what they were saying, it seems clear that the ministers were inclined to talk in terms of the full range of the formal goals of the church with considerable openness as to the means of implementation.

The Members' Perceptions of the Goals. In contrast to the ministers' orientation, the majority of the members mentioned the recruitment of members, the raising of funds, and the construction of a physical plant as the chief goals of the developing congregation.

"The emphasis was on drawing in members, bringing persons into the church. We spread the word through friends. They came in by the handfuls. But the original leaders wore out from responsibility. They weren't building leadership for the future. The congregation thought only of itself in the building campaign."

"Letting the neighbors know we were in the process of organizing. We had too few members. . . . After organizing we had to get a place to meet, get the building up."

"[The main goal of the early congregation was] to build a physical meeting place. There was a lack of money. There had to be. People were pressed with their own problems and establishment. Few new people are automatic tithers."

"Early we were looking anxiously for money to get out of the basement into new quarters. We wanted a space for our own so we could grow. We didn't feel we could grow where we were."

Over three fourths of the respondents referred to the matters of membership, building, and finances as the goals of the developing congregation. Only one fourth of them made any reference to other aspects of the formal goals of the congregation as being important at the outset, and half of this minority were members of the congregation described in Chapter 8 as "a deviant case." This minority felt that an expression of mission through some kind of service to the community, or intensive study by members as to the meaning of their faith, were the primary goals of the congregation at the start. Thus the majority of the members (who eventually became leaders) saw their role in the congregation as one of providing the external equipment or tools for whatever else was to transpire.

Furthermore, their reasons for emphasizing these survival goals were not much related to theological considerations. Their arguments taken together were circular. They felt a building was needed in order to attract new members; that increasing membership made a building mandatory; even that membership recruitment had to be emphasized in order to finance a building.[40] Their understanding was oriented to the normative patterns of congregational life that they had experienced, rather than to the values which are to be expressed through these patterns.[41] Or at the least, the values were only implicit and never quite came to the surface.

Conflict Among the Members. There were also differences in understanding among the members. Some of these differences had to do explicitly with the goals of the congregation and resulted in the withdrawal of some early members, especially those with a fundamentalist position. One of the frequent points of contention was the question whether the congregation should be a relatively closed group serving only the dedicated or whether it should be open to all with only minimal requirements and a broad program, a question bearing directly on the understanding of the nature of the church.

Other differences among the members had to do with matters somewhat less directly related to theological positions, but still not mundane. They concerned the nature of the worship services, the type of church school curriculum, the content of adult study programs, and the amount of social activity among other things.

Finally, there were differences of opinion on matters that were rather strictly technical. The question of how much the building was to cost, its architectural style, types of publicity, and the organization of committees were raised at different times. The one tie between affairs of finance and theological assumptions had to do with how much of the budget should be given to "benevolences." In each congregation there was a division of opinion about whether the congregation's standard contribution to the work of the larger church organization could be compromised in order to finance a building.[42]

Thus, it is apparent that the developing congregation is not a model of social unity. The disagreements and misunderstandings that it entertains vary in intensity. But they are sufficiently disruptive to make some kind of resolution crucial, and they are sufficiently ingrained to limit severely the kinds of resolutions that are possible.

Causes of the Conflict: Diversity of Backgrounds

Enough has been said about the vagueness of the congregation's statements of its formal goals to make clear the importance of this factor in the conflicts that develop. The other factor that contributes to early conflict is the diversity in the backgrounds of the members. These differences are both qualitative and quantitative. The qualitative differences are seen in the various levels of religious sophistication represented in the early congregation; the quantitative differences have to do with both variety and extent of the members' experience in religious groups.

The kind of conflict that follows from the diversity as to quality of religious understanding is seen most clearly in the misunderstandings that occur between the minister and most of the members, although theological sophistication is not necessarily limited to the minister. The tendency is for the more sophisticated to adopt a diffuse view of what it means to be a member of the church, while the less sophisticated are inclined to relate their religious obligations to the organized church and to a popular moralism. This kind of disjunction of understandings can occur, for example, where new members of a congregation include some persons who were active in college student groups, and others whose main experience has been in a small-town congregation. To locate a specific point of conflict, one need only consider the kind of church education material that would please both groups.

On the quantitative side, there are differences in amount of background in the church, and in the kinds of experience the members have had. Some of the members join a new congregation as their first experience in the church. Others have formerly served as officers in another place. There are also differences in the denominations from which the members come; under comity arrangements, the most convenient congregation for them may not be the same as the one in which they had most of their training. Thus someone is likely to be upset because the procedures of the new congregation differ from those he is used to. The wider the range of backgrounds represented, the more likely it is that there will be difficulties in reaching decisions about procedures.

The effect of diversity in backgrounds on the congregation is strongly felt among the earliest members, the charter members. This is the group which sets the tone for the subsequent development of the congregation. Therefore, the manner in which the charter members are brought together is very important. There are several methods of starting new congregations which can be called Single Colony, Multiple Colony, and Accidental Approach.

The Single Colony. The single colony is begun by the efforts of a group that had formerly been in a single nearby congregation. Because of changes in the area, and perhaps in the size of the colonizing congregation, it is decided that the church must make some attempt to serve a new section. The group of members who are actually involved may be determined by the location of their residences or strictly on a volunteer basis. However, the process of deciding to undertake the development of a new congregation is likely to be a deliberate one, and the length of time required makes this approach less efficient than others in an area that is rapidly growing.

The single-colony method does have some distinct advantages. If the idea has come from within the original congregation rather than from one of the denomination's agencies, there may be a keener sense of mission among those involved. And if the colony is based on volunteers there is likely to be a higher sense of dedication than in other forms of gathering personnel. The single colony also has prospects of ease of communication, a stable base for planning, and perhaps a pool of competent leaders, as a result of the members' mutual experience in another congregation.

However, the minimization of diversity in the single colony also has a disadvantage. Because the early members of the new congregation have all come from the same former congregation there may be a tendency to carry over its patterns. At the same time, one of the reasons members volunteer to help found a new congregation is their dissatisfaction with their present congregation. Thus it is possible that there can be creative elements within the single colony.

The Multiple Colony. A multiple colony is made up of groups from several nearby churches who contribute to the effort of organizing a new congregation. Its diversity is likely to be greater than that of a single colony. And because the diversity is limited, there is a greater danger of the formation of factions within the congregation. There is the constant possibility that communications within the congregation will highlight the differences between the several backgrounds represented and that strong tensions will build up between them when there is disagreement on important issues. This possibility is enhanced where the contributing congregations have slightly different orientations (as happens in many cases) and where the colonies are composed on the basis of residence rather than from volunteers.

The multiple colony has the advantage of perhaps making more experienced personnel available to the new congregation than do other approaches, and of bringing together several orientations which can broaden the perspectives of the group. Like the single colony, the multiple colony requires considerable time to be effected and is limited to those situations where there is sufficient cooperation between nearby congregations.

The Accidental Approach. "Accidental" is used here in a strictly descriptive way and no value judgment should be inferred. This approach depends on the minister's ability to attract members to the new congregation from among the persons who happen to be residing in the geographic area which the congregation is to serve. He usually proceeds by some kind of census of the area and then attempts to develop a core of members from among those who respond with interest. As a result, the composite character of the new congregation is an accidental consequence of the qualifications of the persons who happen to move into the area. This approach lacks even the modest opportunity to determine the composition of the earliest group that is present in the other approaches, and increases the possibility of a dearth of leaders.

The accidental approach is the one most widely used in new church development. (In some cases it is modified by the addition of members contributed by nearby congregations.) It is especially applicable to rapidly growing

areas into which denominational agencies can send an
organizing minister to take advantage of the expanding
number of the momentarily unchurched. The decision to
begin a new congregation usually comes from an agency's
awareness of housing developments and population
growth and the assumption that the new residents will
need churches, rather than from a grass-roots movement
of nearby church members. As a result, the sense of
mission among the early members gathered in this way
may differ from that of the colonies.

At the same time that the accidental approach produces a congregation with a clear geographic unity, it
also incorporates a greater diversity among members than
the other approaches. This diversity has the advantage of
providing a variety of perspectives on how the congregation should proceed, and it reduces the likelihood of the
development of factions based on members' prior affilia-
tions. It also has the disadvantage of giving rise to
inhibiting conflict partly because of difficulties of communication. However, it should be noted that difficulties
in communication can also lead to a deliberate examination of the congregation's intentions, an examination that
is often missing where a greater ease of communications
enables members to take a great deal for granted.

The method by which the charter members of the new
congregation are gathered is particularly important since
the agencies that plan new churches have some control
over it. If, for example, reducing the diversity of backgrounds in the early congregation can help to reduce
conflict about its goals, it may be worthwhile to shape
the initial efforts in that direction. The more stable a
front the earliest members present to the subsequent
members, the less likely that uncongenial persons will

seek affiliation and the more likely that the original emphases can be maintained.

Resolution of the Conflict: Deferred Goals

There are a number of ways in which new congregations react to conflict. In some of them the majority rules and essentially purges itself of dissenting members. In others where the power is more evenly balanced but the contestants are more passionate, there can be a split into several new congregations. However, the conflicts that appear in the early stages of the life of the developing congregation are usually resolved at least temporarily by deferring the consideration of some primary interests. The substance of the resolution, around survival goals, will be examined in detail in the next chapter. A prior question is that of why the congregation caught up in conflict does not inevitably disintegrate before it ever gets started. Why do members have the patience to stay with it and reach any form of resolution?

First, it should be pointed out that there is a consensus within the congregation even at the earliest stages. This consensus centers around the most common activities of any church—worship and church school. Whatever the disagreements on doctrinal matters or technical matters, there is a common desire to participate in worship and to have training for the children. Further, these activities, if closely related to Biblical emphases, will be satisfactory to most of the members. In the common participation in worship and in the support of the church school there is the beginning of a feeling of unity in the congregation.

Second, the rehearsal of vaguely stated formal goals in the worship service provides an opportunity for a unanimous consent, even though there may be variations in interpretation of the symbols used. This ecclesiastical symbolism is familiar to the members from Biblical texts, hymns, and church school materials. On one level, it includes such terms as salvation, grace, redemption, discipleship, belief, evangelism, dedication, and blessing. On a level perhaps more contemporary, it includes commitment, mission, concern, dialogue, faith, involvement, authenticity, and community. These symbols are on a plane sufficiently abstract that they can be given content by the concrete experiences of the hearer. As a result, agreement can be found around them in the public rehearsals of the goals.

However, at the same time that these symbols contribute to the unity of the congregation, they may also inhibit clear communication. Some may use the term "mission" to mean the efforts of Christians to promote social justice and reduce conflict, while others think of it as the foreign missions program of the denomination. Some may speak of "redemptive fellowship" to refer to a particular quality of relationship between persons, while to others it simply means the membership of the congregation. Some may think of "outreach" as the church making itself visible by its activities to the world, while others consider it a fancy word for gaining new members. Thus, differences in understanding can be masked by unity in symbolism and the broader meanings reduced to limited ones. In this way, to push the point a bit far, the "equipping of the saints" can become the construction of a physical plant.

Third, where the differences in understanding become apparent, there can be acceptance of the differences through a tacit division of labor. The practical concerns of the congregation become the sphere of some members;

the more abstract ones are left to others.[43] In a way, this is an extension of the tolerant attitude of some members that the minister is often a little less than practical in his ideas. These members may be able to admit that the more diffuse ideas about the goals have a place in the church, but they simply feel that their own talents lie in other directions. While this sort of division of duties contributes to the combining of diverse orientations within the congregation, it can also lead to serious splits which have consequences for the overall program of the church. Where the leaders, for example, take the more limited view, the work of the church can be severely handicapped. One member of a ruling board illustrated this point:

> "[The session] seems often just to go round and round, batting the wind. It deals mostly with the financial business of the church. The session should have more spiritual business to transact, but we just don't ever get into that aspect. There is no reason at all for the session as it now is. A clerk-treasurer is all that's needed. The committees are just window dressing."

Finally, the effect of early conflict in the congregation is minimized by the very newness of the experience. In the earliest stages, nothing has sufficient tradition behind it to appear formalized. Almost any kind of change can be anticipated. Thus, there is not as much keen disappointment for members whose own desires have not been realized immediately in the program. It is possible to find solace in the contemplation of the ideal future.

For those who desire a broader conception of the congregation's mission than is realized in working toward the survival goals, there is an additional rationalization available. The argument that it is necessary to get the

congregation established before it can get down to work
is very compelling. These members are able to defer their
hopes for a more comprehensive approach and to participate in the important but temporary work of insuring the
congregation's survival. The minister in particular must
be able to make use of this rationalization.

These are the ways, then, in which the effect of early
conflict is reduced and consensus is established. These
are the mechanisms which make the continuation of the
congregation possible. The consensus is not the result of
a conscious arbitrating of differences, but rather comes
as an almost "natural" development out of the conditions
in which the developing congregation finds itself. The
consensus enables the members to move, some temporarily and some permanently, toward a resolution of
the goal conflict around survival goals. The conditions
that make any kind of resolution possible have been
examined above; the pressures that make for a resolution
around survival goals are treated in the following chapter.

5

PRESSURES TOWARD AN EMPHASIS ON SURVIVAL

One of the congregations examined in this study was able to achieve considerable "success" without emphasizing survival goals. Whether the other congregations could have altered their orientations and survived is a moot question. However, the fact that congregations facing relatively similar conditions do respond in different ways suggests that it is not inevitable that new congregations develop in the same pattern. It also raises the question of what kind of conditions and factors there are confronting the new congregation that incline it to emphasize survival goals.

In this chapter, the factors that constitute a pressure toward a survival-goal orientation will be described in terms of the system problems to which they are most closely related. It is assumed that any congregation will have to encourage the morale of its members, establish an authority structure, and adapt itself in some ways to its environment. The term "survival goals," as it is used here, means specifically the recruitment and maintenance of members, the raising of funds, and the construction of a building.

Morale: Segmental Participation

The congregation is a voluntary association. As such, it has no assurance that the members will not withdraw when they begin to feel dissatisfied with the congregation. Beyond that, the congregation must provide something of value in order to attract members in the first place. An answer to why persons become members of the congregation is a clue to the kind of program the congregation will have to have in order to maintain their interest. It is important, therefore, to realize that the members of a developing congregation are present for a great variety of reasons.

The largest part of the respondents reported that they (and, in their opinion, others with whom they had contact) had sought out the congregation either because they were looking for friendships or because they wanted their children to have religious training. This kind of motivation has been referred to by other investigators of the religious scene.[44] Others came to the congregation either because church had become a part of their way of life or to find something "worthwhile" in which to participate. Most of the members were vague about what the church meant to them; they seemed to be either reestablishing a part of their past or waiting to see what would happen.

Except for those who are looking for religious training for their children, it is puzzling why the church should be selected over other forms of activity. Gibson Winter admits being mystified about this, but proposes two reasons on a psychological level. First, the kind of activity that the congregation engages in involves the member in a feeling of community. The congregation is of particular value in this regard because it is one of a very few organizations that represents the residential area. It thus enables the member to make contact with his neighbors and to feel that he is living in a community rather than merely a geographic sector. Second, Winter suggests that activity in the congregation may serve the Protestant as penitential activity for the expiation of guilt. The willingness of members to be involved in drudge-type work for the congregation may be a rather economical way to rid themselves of a sense of sinfulness.[45] The former of these suggestions at least is quite reasonable, given the lack of organizations in the suburbs in general, and in new suburbs in particular.

All the evidence seems to point to the fact that the members of the developing congregation represent a diversity of motives. Where their reasons do not embrace the whole range of formal goals, they can be called *segmental participants*. This segmental participation is one of the characteristics of the developing congregation. Persons are encouraged to join, even though they have a limited interest, in the hope that continued contact will lead them to more complete commitment. Indeed, this tactic has been given explicit expression and recommended as the best way the local congregation can make itself felt in the community.[46] The acceptance of segmental participation has two consequences for the congregation. On the one hand, it forces the congregation into the operation of a broad program in order to satisfy the diverse interests of its members. And on the other hand, it places in membership a group of persons who will have more concern for the survival of the congregation (and the program in which they are interested) than its attainment of its formal goals. Thus, the attempt to satisfy a membership that has a wide range of motives and interests is one factor that inclines the congregation to resolve goal conflict in favor of survival goals.

A second pressure toward survival goals is in the contrast they give by their concreteness to the abstract formal goals. Members are able to understand what it means to get members, or raise money, or put up a building, but they are not so clear about the general mission. They are more inclined to accept some clear and limited task than to commit themselves to the uncertain demands of leading a youth group, teaching church school, or serving on a committee the title of which does not specify its job.

Indeed, there is considerable enthusiasm generated around the possibility of seeing the developing fruits of one's labor. The visibility of the efforts of the developing congregation in moving toward a realization of the survival goals is one of the chief contributors to group morale in that early period. It becomes a driving force both in the planning and in the work. Nearly all of the respondents would agree with this.

> "There was a sense of pride and excitement at getting the building under way. The men got together to do the building. It was a thrill to see our church being built, to see it go up stage by stage. I remember even being thrilled at watching them pour concrete. It makes you want to work for it more."

> "The people had a will to work together to build the church. You got that impression from working with them. We had work details every Saturday. It was hard work—from pouring the concrete, to laying pipe, and putting up shingles. We did everything but the concrete finishing ourselves. It's a mistake now that the congregation has nothing to do."

> "The congregation was new and different and a challenge. There was life in the church from the beginning.

We got caught up in starting it. We invited our friends.
It seemed to click right through. As the members began
to multiply we began to feel a responsibility for them."

Furthermore, the enthusiasm was not only around the
visibility of the results of their labor, but also at the visibility of other members' dedication. It was possible to be
aware of the amount of time that others put into the
work, to know that they were sacrificing evenings and
weekends for this thing. This visibility of progress and
dedication are not found to the same extent or at least
so dramatically in the other jobs of the congregation. And,
they are almost totally lacking when the work is defined
in terms of the members' activity in their daily lives in
the everyday world. Thus survival goals or the activities
associated with them can be a very real source of integration, both in the anticipation and in the actual work.
However, the integration that is based on them is a
limited one, and has serious consequences for the congregation at a later stage.

Authority

The necessity of effecting a division of labor within
the congregation and establishing a system of authority
positions also advances the seeming importance of survival goals. We have already seen that there is often a
kind of tacit understanding that the members will concern themselves with practical matters and relegate religious considerations to the minister. Beyond that there
are pressures on the minister himself, coming from several directions, which force him toward adopting survival
goals as a resolution for several different problems.

The Minister: Insecurity. The minister is the key man
in the developing congregation. In many cases he is its

only visible representative for a while. Whatever leadership is developed depends upon his efforts. At the same time, he is responsible to denominational agencies for what goes on in the congregation, and he must be responsive to the members whose needs he is committed to serve. Under pressure from two sides, he is certainly a man in the middle.[47]

The new-church minister is faced with the mammoth task of organizing his congregation from the ground up; the main work of educating the congregation and training personnel falls to him; he is called upon from the earliest stages to serve as counselor for the many family problems that arise in the young suburbs; and he must carry on the normal ecclesiastical functions of his position. In sum, he must pursue all the usual tasks that a minister in an established parish has, and in addition must devote considerable time to the extra work that goes with stimulating and coordinating the activities of a new organization. In the midst of so many claims, the minister can be excused perhaps for not mounting an intense effort to clarify the abstract theological imperatives of the church, or to moderate a continual debate about the congregation's best expression of its mission.

However, the minister is not only constrained by the amount of work; he is also limited by the expectations of the members. The main pressure on him is to service the many jobs that are visible to the congregation. Those which are more diffuse or have less visible "payoffs" often take on lesser significance in the eyes of his parishioners.[48] Thus, the efforts to assess the needs of the community and their relevance to theological imperatives may appear to the member to be inconsequential. Teaching small but intense theological discussion groups may appear to be of less moment than operations that affect directly larger numbers of persons, such as preparing anecdote-peppered sermons or making brief social calls to each member family. As a result, the minister is pressured into devoting his time to tasks with more immediate and obvious repercussions, and to neglecting the task of giving greater consideration to the translation of the formal goals.

The minister of a developing congregation is likely to be particularly sensitive to pressures from those to whom he is responsible because of his insecurity. The organizing minister (who not necessarily but usually becomes the first minister of the newly formed congregation) is usually unfamiliar with the situation in which he will be working. Because he typically comes from a different area he is not familiar with the conditions of the community. He knows few, if any, of the members of the governing bodies of the denomination in the area or the officials of its agencies. His fellow ministers are not likely to know his work. He is not acquainted with his future parishioners. As a result, he is known only through the work he does and is under great pressure to succeed. His insecurity, considering that his subsequent career may depend upon what he does, is perhaps higher than in any other form of the ministry.[49] With the combination of the pressures and the insecurity, there is probably an inclination in the most resolute of men to play it safe, avoid risks, and make sure of success.[50] It is not difficult to understand how a man in such a position might temporarily capitulate in a conflict about goals and direct the congregation to the tasks of survival.

Lay Authority: Specialized Leadership. The primary channel through which the minister reaches the congregation with policy decisions is the board of lay leaders.

Except for a few matters relating to the ritual life of the congregation, these leaders are peers of the minister in responsibility for the direction of the congregation. Their power is such that the minister cannot alone balance it. Thus it is important that the leaders themselves have a sound idea of the congregation's goals.

However, there are two factors that affect the understanding of the leaders. The first is that they are likely to have had little experience in leading a congregation: suburban residents are usually young persons, and persons who have been on the move. The second factor that affects the understanding of the leadership groups is the criterion by which they are elected to their positions. There is a tendency to select those persons who can be helpful because of their special skills rather than on the basis of their religious maturity.[51] In most of the congregations, the men who were identified as having been especially influential in the developing congregations were described as having been of great help in handling loans, in arranging for contractors, and in securing insurance. Thus, the very consideration of a building program can bring into prominence persons who will be inclined to emphasize it. These persons whose counsel is solicited for specialized interests are elected to positions which entitle them to make policy for the congregation on all matters. The result can be a lack of religious understanding in leaders, and a tendency to push toward survival goals. The effects of such leadership can be felt even after the congregation is established.

> "The session doesn't really see these problems [of theological differences]. . . . Many of them are too young; they don't have experience. . . . A number of session members were chosen because they were good executives."

*The Denominational Bureaus: Unanticipated Conse-
quences.* Finally, but not of least significance in the pressures toward an emphasis on survival goals, there is the
influence of the relevant agencies in the bureaucracy.
The organizing minister is usually called to his post by an
agency that guarantees his salary for a limited time. Thus
the minister is paid to bring about results generally in
line with the agency's desires. The agency makes recommendations about how the work should progress, and
while the aims would be expressed in theological terms,
the recommendations are in terms of periods of time until
a minimum number of members is gathered, a budget is
established, and the first units of the building are up.[52]
These recommendations serve as indicators of the progress of the new congregation and failure to fulfill them
can be interpreted as showing something is wrong with
the congregation. In part the bureaucratic stress on statistical performance is a result of the difficulty of defining
and measuring a congregation's progress in terms of its
formal goals. The agency falls back on measures related
more closely to survival goals and by its procedures con-
veys to the new-church ministers, whether intentionally
or not, the impression that statistical measures are of
primary importance. The intention of the agency is to
maintain some kind of order in its overseeing of numerous
churches, but the result is a subtle pressure toward survival goals.

That this pressure is not appreciated by the ministers
can be seen in some of their comments. The most statistically successful minister of those studied said:

"I liked the freedom of an unstructured situation where
the work isn't hampered by tradition. But underlying all
the new-church work is the idea of an investment paying
off. It forces us to make unrealistic expectations of

people who have an inadequate understanding of the church. There is a lack of time for the new-church pastor to nurture the members. The building is assumed to be important."

Another minister gave this opinion about the policies of the boards that affected his situation:

"The whole mission of the church in new-church development might be evaluated. We tend to extend the cultural structure and ethos, the land, the building, the program, rather than the calling out of a people to *mission in the area*. Granted a church needs a building and program facilities—but if the mission becomes that in fact, the rest will take shape and be formed to that mission."

Another suggested these changes in policy to presbytery:

"There should be greater emphasis on new-member training and integration so that all unite and can freely accept the goals of the group. . . . Sufficient financial backing by presbytery to enable the officers to accept only those who subscribe to the discipline of the church. . . . Less commitment to land and buildings, and more counseling and guidance by higher judicatories so that early in the congregation's life basic moneys can go into *program*."

The substance of these statements is that there is indeed recognizable pressure from the boards on the new-church ministers, and that this pressure is instrumental in diverting their attention from problems, such as membership training and effective programming, which they feel are important.

The ministers also feel pressure from another source, though it may be channeled through their denominational agencies. Where a denomination has been granted a franchise to operate in a particular area under a comity agreement with an interdenominational board, there is pressure on the minister to develop a congregation as rapidly as possible so that the potential members in the area can be contacted before noncooperative religious groups move in. If the congregation does not develop along traditional lines and grow with the population, the interdenominational board may be inclined to be more restrictive in its dealings with the denomination in the future.

Taken together, the pressures from agencies above and from the members and lay leaders within the congregation make a marked impression on the minister. Especially because he is in a very insecure position, he will understandably be inclined to take survival goals very seriously, and it is not difficult to understand how he might temporarily compromise his dedication to the formal goals.

Adaptation to the Parish Area: Harvesttime?

Finally, there are conditions of the environment of the developing congregation that can help to divert its attention from formal goals to survival goals. There are at least two characteristics of the suburbs which attract it in this direction, and one which hinders its pursuit of formal goals.

First, the suburbs in which developing congregations are located are likely to show a rapid population growth. This means there is a great number of potential members, from one point of view, or persons in need of the church, from another. The former view makes the work of membership recruitment highly rewarding; the latter makes it difficult to discourage anyone who wishes to join the congregation for whatever reasons. Whether they are taken in eagerly, or from a feeling of obligation, the new members because of their number create new problems.

They make proper assimilation into the church more difficult, and they force consideration of expansion. The result is usually a more intense focus on survival goals, and a neglect of the formal goals. One member reflected on that period in his own congregation in this way:

> "I'm generally pessimistic about a group attaining success if that is its goal. In the days of three worship services there was pressure to get out of the small chapel. The minister appeared to be satisfied with the job being done with the facilities, but it was argued that he would have to work less hard with a new building. There was a desire to be self-sustaining and to make use of the potential money we had. This had been a mission church that wanted to be up on its benevolence giving, which had the support of the minister. But new people brought pressure for a sanctuary. We were able to get a loan without 50 percent in hand (which should have been done without decreasing other funds). It distressed me that basic responsibilities were sacrificed for the building."

Second, the new suburb is without any other bases for social integration. Many of the residents are eager to find a means to get acquainted with their neighbors and to get a sense of the community.[53] This means the congregation is likely to get a lot of attention, and get it from persons whose interest is not particularly in its formal goals. Both the pressure of numbers, and the segmental interest of most of them, contribute to the congregation's interest in survival goals (particularly the building) and its lack of interest in the full range of formal goals.

Third, because the suburbs are usually so homogeneous in terms of the characteristics of the residents and of the facilities, there tends to be a lack of concrete opportunities in the immediate community for the expression of such service as the congregation might consider. Here people are for the most part healthy and affluent; there is not much visible poverty, crime, racial tension, deterioration, or even old age. As long as the congregation is inclined to stay fairly closely within its own neighborhood, there will not be any dramatic needs to attract its attention and turn its interests outward. To find such opportunities for service would take a special effort which at this point is restrained by a host of other demands.

The Character of the Developing Congregation

The developing congregation is an association with great hopes, high enthusiasm, and a variety of understandings about what it should do. The concrete activities of worship and church school are the starting point for its corporate life. Beyond that, conflicts within the congregation about further activities force a compromise about its proximate goals. Conditions within the new congregation pressure it toward a resolution of these conflicts around survival goals.

The conflicts are essentially a question of priorities—that is, which of the formal goals should be pursued at this early time. The resolution is in favor of those directly related to the survival of the congregation as a social entity. Activity toward survival goals satisfies those who are interested in concrete and limited tasks, those who feel the tasks are at least necessary if not primary, and those who have only a segmental interest in the congregation. The survival goals are thus a means of integrating the diverse orientations in the developing congregation. Further, where there are no clear alternatives for selecting leaders, the concrete survival tasks provide a criterion. The minister feels pressure from his members and from

the agencies above him to present visible evidence that
he is busy and that his efforts are effective. He is faced
with too many jobs to handle adequately and must make
a decision about priorities in his own role. The insecurity
of his position inclines him toward a temporary emphasis
on survival goals. Finally, the suburban context offers no
clear opportunities for translating the congregation's goal
of service into concrete efforts; the congregation serves
by welcoming residents to the church as a center for
community socializing.

The formal goals are not rejected out of hand. Some
feel they are adequately expressed in the work of the
survival goals. Others feel they are postponed in the interest of unity and getting under way until a more propi-
tious time. The subsequent character of the developing
congregation shows the effects of this resolution.

Community: High Enthusiasm. The congregation is
organized around the worship service. In this there is a
censensus of the members. The structures of the group
are those prescribed by the governmental pattern of the
denomination, but the selection of officers is often on the
basis of criteria extraneous to the formal goals of the congregation. The informal life or atmosphere of the congregation is one of its most striking features. It shows a
high degree of enthusiasm and unity, almost a state of
euphoria. It is still relatively small and is more open-
ended than cliquish. Many close personal ties are made,
especially among the original members, and the developing congregation comes close to realizing the community
that its formal goals recommend. The one caveat about
this community is that it is founded to a large extent on
the temporary activities connected with the survival

goals. Thus there is a suggestion of spuriousness about it. There is under the surface of the community a number of incipient crises that are only temporarily obscured by the enthusiasm of building a church.

Nurture: Share the Work. The developing congregation begins a church school program very early. And because of the small number involved at the start, most members are active in some position of responsibility. Both of these characteristics are relevant to the formal goal of nurture. However, the congregations are inclined to neglect, or to decline in their original interest in, adult education. Furthermore, the responsibilities that are exercised by such a large proportion of the members are usually related to the congregation's internal life rather than to a broader form of service as an expression of the church. They are inclined to see their contributions to the congregation, or their financial contributions to the larger church organization, as the fulfillment of their obligations. The members become the servants of the local congregation, identify themselves with the larger church, but retain an extra-curricular view of their individual responsibilities. Insofar as this is the case, the congregation is negligent in the expression of its formal goals.

Service: Internal Focus. The developing congregation is partial in realizing this aspect of its formal goals also. While much effort goes into the recruitment of members, there is little or no interest in service to the nonchurched in other forms. The congregation sees its encouragement of affiliation as evangelism and in the main internalizes its attention. Even the money that it contributes to benevolences is seen more as an indicator of the congregation's fulfilling its obligations than as a means for concrete service. It is probably this internalization of attention that is the outstanding characteristic of the developing congregation. It does not reluctantly carry out its survival goals of necessity as it pursues its formal goals; rather, it tends to ignore the formal goals as it goes about insuring its survival.

For the most part, the developing congregation is oblivious to the sacrificial mode that should pervade its work. Caution and good business sense are likely to be the prevailing attitudes. The avoidance of risk is rightly or wrongly considered to be "good stewardship."

6

THE DEVELOPED CONGREGATION: STALEMATE

The developed congregation is not so much characterized by a sigh of relief that the dirty work is done as by
a feeling of being let down. The unity of effort that was
woven of diverse interests in the developing congregation comes unraveled when the immediate pressure is
off, and there is a loss of momentum when tasks that once
seemed like such a challenge are accomplished. The congregation in the "developed" stage has reached that point
which the minister anticipated as the time for evaluation
and turning to a fuller service of the congregation's formal goals. It is the time about which the members had
visions and hopes. The concrete changes are that there
is a physical plant in existence with only minor improve-
ments to be made, the budget has been consistently met
in spite of several close calls, and the general turmoil that
comes with a constant influx of new members has abated.
This is the point at which the members can begin to
assume that the congregation is here to stay, and to ask,
"What now?"

It has been assumed by the minister, and by some of
those members who had particular interests that they
wanted to implement, that this would be the occasion

for changing the congregation's direction in some way or other. The deferred interests were several. There were those who desired a turning outward to the world in some kind of significant service. Others were interested in more sophisticated theological discussions or in concentrated study of the Bible. Some members hoped that the congregation would settle down into a stable group and develop the kind of homely acquaintance that goes with small-town churches. Others were inclined to more interesting programs and a fuller social life. But for the largest number of members, the work of the congregation had become all that could be expected, and any anticipation of more to come was vague and undefined. Further, the maintenance of services of worship and church school were to them ample justification for the congregation's existence. The developed congregation has not lost its diversity of orientations, but only a specific kind of survival goal.

The result of these developments is that there is resistance to changing the congregation's orientation, and pressures for maintaining the *status quo*. While the two kinds of conditions are similar in some respects, they will be treated separately here. In this chapter, we will deal with the factors which are inimical to bringing about change in the congregation. In the next chapter, we will consider the factors that incline the congregation to continue the kind of program it already has.

The conditions making for resistance to change are the loss of enthusiasm, especially on the part of leaders, the rise of controversy, and dissatisfaction with the minister. Although these factors themselves do not create pressure for maintaining the *status quo*, they tend to inhibit discussion and lower morale, both of which indirectly support continuation rather than change. The existing program largely consists of the running of the church school, the maintenance of special-interest activities, and the technical aspects of managing the organization as well as the activities associated with the rituals. Upkeep has superseded construction as the mode of thinking.

The Loss of Enthusiasm

One of the marks of the developing congregation was a great idealism in looking toward the future; the mark of the developed congregation is an idealization of the past. Those persons who were connected with the congregation in its earliest stages, and who are for the most part now in leadership positions, seem to remember a charismatic association, a community both exciting and personal.

"It was a terrific group that started. It had a missionary zeal. It was a terrific experience. We wrestled with problems and had heated discussions but we always parted with the wonderful feeling that something was being accomplished, and that we were together in the feeling of a job to be done."

"The beginnings were electric in the steering committee. It had the same spirit as you think of in the New Testament church. Some persons had no intention of joining the church, but said they 'just got booted out here.' There was a spontaneous development."

"The minister became a friend to us. There was a great excitement among the nucleus. We were meeting in a garage. It seemed so unusual. There was a communion among the group immediately. So much of our lives then was an experiment. We had to learn everything."

As was noted before, however, much of this enthusiasm was a result of the unity of the members around the con-

crete tasks connected with survival goals. There was a
clear kind of mission before them, a church to be built,
a congregation to be established. They were taking part
in the creation of something that was inherently, if incom-
prehensively, good. This linking of the early enthusiasm
with the survival tasks has been realized by some of the
members.

> "We're not enthusiastic now. I felt an uplift when the
> minister of music came this year. But the church has
> become big business to some members of the session.
> The present lull may be due to the end of the building
> program. You know, there is more excitement about the
> physical."

> "I was enthusiastic about the building and furnishings.
> I knew there was a real desperate need. You like to do
> things under those circumstances. We could get more
> enthusiastic. There will be a reburst of enthusiasm with
> the [new] pews. Card-table chairs are too cold."

> "Some people are active for several years, then disappear
> when church work becomes busywork. We begin to lose
> sight of the goals. Some work is not utilized and seems
> like a waste of time."

Thus one reason for the loss of enthusiasm in the developed congregation is the completion of the limited,
tangible goals related to the growth of the congregation.
Beside them, many of the tasks that follow seem to be of
little concrete value, and are rejected as busywork. This
attachment of enthusiasm to the progress of the physical
plant in particular is highlighted by the several suggestions that such additions as rugs for the sanctuary, or
pews, would regenerate the spirit of the congregation.

A second reason for the loss of enthusiasm has to do
with the rapid increase in the number of members. The

intimacy of the original group is lost with the arrival of many new people, and they come so fast that there is little chance of adequately assimilating them. This results in the leaders feeling helpless in the midst of a crowd of strangers, a kind of questioning of the motives of the new members, and a loss of a sense of close community.

> "There is a feeling of fellowship among the older members, but we can't bring the new people into it. Some who were very active before have dropped out. We don't know why."

> "There have been a great many more people with the growth of the church. It's more complex, more impersonal. We need a maturing process for the new members. At one time we had a very dynamic outreach program. Dedication is lower now."

> "There is not enough opportunity to get to know people. There is a larger number of unchurched people coming with a great variety of backgrounds. Not so many Presbyterians. There is a lack of depth of knowledge."

The effect of the growth of the membership on the intimacy of the original group is increased where there is also a suspicion that the new members are not really committed to the congregation as the original members were.

> "After the building there was a flood of new people who diluted the membership. It curtailed our ability to know people. It was an influx not only of new residents, but of people who had just been waiting to join. There was a slight resentment perhaps. Some questioned why the people didn't come and join in the work before the building was up."

> "There has been an inability to get the spirit, the missionary zeal, of the charter members to the new people. We haven't been able to analyze this. There are three

factions in the church now: fundamentalists, moderates, and liberals. We interpreted these divisions at our [planning] conference as a spiritual 'low.' "

Thus the loss of the dramatic physical tasks and the dilution of the original membership make for a loss of enthusiasm among the older members, the leadership stratum. An important question that follows from all this is, why do the older members continue to work with the congregation if they have lost their enthusiasm and feel there is a lack of dedication? The answer in many cases is that they feel a sense of obligation. They see themselves as responsible for the decisions that got the congregation into debt for buildings and equipment and now they are bound to stay with it until those matters are taken care of. These are the kinds of responses made to a question about why they continue in the congregation:

"I need to stay until I feel the church is set, or jelled. It's a desire to be there until the immediate goals have been met. The building program more than anything else. We have committed ourselves, even though some things are less to our liking than in other congregations."

"It's a matter of duty. I don't want to let them down. I feel a need for tuning up my own spiritual life. I don't know that it's helped. It doesn't seem to be alive with spiritual life now."

"Just a feeling of duty. I feel obligated. I wish I could say it's a call from the Lord. I'm disillusioned with the church now. I continue because of hope and obligation."

It seems clear from these statements that a number of the respondents would like to see change in the congregations, but that they are dispirited rather than optimistic about the prospects. This can be interpreted as evidence to support the contention that there are overwhelming conditions in the congregations that work counter to change. These conditions include commitments to the ongoing program which though not sufficient is still judged to be necessary, and the difficulty in finding consensus as to the specific kinds of changes to be sought. The respondents gave quite diverse answers about the kinds of programs they felt should be introduced or expanded. The loss of enthusiasm may be due in part to this kind of pessimism. Insofar as the conditions that depress the members are due to an early emphasis on survival goals, we can say that this emphasis works to sap enthusiasm both directly and indirectly.

If the loss of enthusiasm is in part the result of the loss of tangible evidence of progress, then it is valid to inquire if the formal goals cannot be expressed in terms of some tangible tasks. The answer is that they can, but that the translation is a process which requires the leadership of the minister who is not in a good position to carry it out. He is beleaguered by the demands of running the church and is not free to introduce such changes as he might prefer. The kind of work that would be required to implement the more diffuse goals is usually personal and private. This kind of activity can be shared for the most part only in small groups, and it is precisely in these that the minister is not able to spend his time because of demands of tasks relating directly to larger numbers of members.[54]

In addition, there are inherent structural blocks to the translation of the formal goals. The new emphases would have to do with creating community within the congregation, furthering adult education, and individual initiative in the expression of mission, and the emphasizing of corporate service to the needs of the society. The com-

munity aspect has been sapped by growth and is difficult
to illustrate; intensive adult education interests so few as
to make the spending of the minister's time on it dubious;
individual activity outside the congregation is difficult to
share except in small groups; and uncovering the needs
of the suburban society requires dedication and special
effort. Without the leadership of the minister and the
support of lay leaders, this kind of change is difficult to
bring about at all.

Reemergence of Conflict

It was pointed out above that one of the functions of
the survival goals for the developing congregation is to
provide a basis of unity that would reconcile conflict
about goals among the members. With the near completion of the tasks connected with these survival goals,
there is a chance for a reemergence of such differences.
While it may have been hoped by the minister that in
the course of building the congregation such differences
would be resolved, the evidence is that such is not the
case. For the most part, the differences arise with a new
vigor born of the fact that the proponents have contributed a great deal to the congregation and feel that
they have quite a stake in it. If the conflicts had been
aired at the outset, it is likely that one faction or another
would have left and in so doing removed a part of the
pressure to compromise on the primacy of survival goals.
Because the encounter was deferred, the contending parties now share at least a determination that the opponent
shall not have the victory.

The content of the conflict is more wholly theological
than it was in the developing congregation. And it
centers, ironically, on the understanding of the nature

of the church including the interpretations of its formal goals. There are controversies about whether or not the church should be of service to the society, whether it should support the councils of churches, what it should teach, what agencies are worthy of its financial support. Although such questions can be raised in any congregation, there is a tendency for disputants in the new churches to coalesce in two or three factions that share the same position on a number of topics. This tendency is especially divisive where the congregation was begun by the multiple colony method; in this case the lines are sharply drawn and the members who entered later are caught, confused, in the middle.

In most of the congregations, there was some kind of very general division between what might be called "liberals" and "conservatives," though these designations are not quite accurate.

"There is a tension between the ideas of a money-raising club vs. an exclusive unit of people: liberals vs. conservatives, socialites vs. fundamentalists. The former want to gather everybody into a social group, have much activity, and make lots of money, though the ends aren't certain. The latter want a program that is isolated from the community at large."

One of the specific areas of controversy that often comes up concerns money.

"There is questioning about the one-to-two ratio [one dollar for benevolences for every two spent in the local budget] in missions giving. Some would like to see missions on a more individualistic basis. At the present time much of it goes to the Office of Church and Society in this country. We need to get a closer feeling for foreign missions."

Another area, touched on in the quote above, that has become increasingly a matter of debate, is the church's involvement in social action. Four of six ministers in this study had been outspoken on social issues, and three of them had been under severe criticism for it by a faction in their congregations. Even where the minister tries to avoid such issues, there can be tension because of them.

> "There is an informal controversy about the John Birch Society's infiltrating the congregation and starting a whispering campaign that might cause it to explode. Also, on the Proposition 14 [California constitutional amendment that made so-called fair housing laws illegal] issue. The minister is afraid the congregation might explode on that issue."

When such controversies are a matter of give-and-take within the congregation, and where there is no crystallization of sentiment into contending factions, they can be a sign of vitality. However, in most of the cases studied the period of the developing congregation did not see a reconciliation of the several factions that disagreed at the beginning. Rather, they continued sometimes by explicit means.

> "There are two cliques, different in background. The people who thought alike went to departments that followed their view. One group centered in the Mission and Christian Education Departments. The other is largely in Worship and Building and Grounds. The job now is to get these orientations scattered around."

> "The fight over the [theological content of the] curriculum material was very big, and the crisis has increased. There is a decided division in the church now with one faction led by one of the assistant ministers. It's between the middle-of-the-road, Presbyterian, Republican, constitutional theology, and a modern theology that accepts

almost anything. A minority is strongly liberal, a larger minority is strongly conservative, and the vast majority literally don't know what they believe."

It is the convincing urgency of the survival tasks in the developing congregation that makes possible a moratorium on such discussions until after the congregation is established. It is the entrenchment of the contending parties as a result of their contributions to these tasks, and the factionalization as a result of natural affinities during the service of these tasks, that enables the ensuing conflict to result in a standoff.

Dissatisfaction with the Minister

The person who is in the only position to mediate such conflicts as they develop is the minister. Unfortunately, he is likely to come under fire himself. Whether it is a matter of the loss of momentum of the congregation or a change in the minister himself, it appears to be a rule that after the most critical stages of the congregation's struggle for survival are past, there will be an outbreak of criticism of the minister. Almost without exception, this criticism comes from a small minority of the congregation. However, its effect is to undermine further the unity of the congregation, and to deepen the minister's insecurity. Where the minister is under fire from one quarter, his role as an arbitrator is less effective.

The criticisms of the minister have to do either with his theological orientation or with his effectiveness as a dynamic person in attracting new members. Both of the appraisals seem to be made in terms of his preaching, perhaps because this is where the minister is most visible to most of the members. Many of the criticisms suggest that the minister has in some way changed his orienta-

tion, and in some cases this is a fact. Once the congregation had been stabilized, the ministers tried in various
ways to bring about an evaluation of the congregations'
programs. The sermon was one means of communicating
with the congregation about possible avenues for new
commitments. But the change in tone disturbed some
members.

> "We have had strong pulpit persons in our background.
> The Lord may be wanting us to seek our meat in other
> areas than the sermon. We have to think through and
> see why we should stay. We can stay home and read
> and feel more blessed than by going to the sermon.
> The minister leans more to social-education-and-action
> type sermons."

> "[The minister] began to compromise on doctrine. We
> were praying that [he] would return to basic principles.
> I don't think [he] ever really changed in himself, but
> he seemed to begin to leave Biblical standards."

The other focus of criticism is on the minister's charismatic qualities, especially in the pulpit. Members will
admit that he is friendly and well liked, that he is a good
organizer, that he is respected as an adviser and counselor, but if he does not attract new members to his services, there is suspicion that he is not doing his job.
These attitudes are clear evidence that the survival goals
(in this case, recruitment of members) can be used as
criteria by which to judge congregational leadership, and
even the minister.

> "The evangelical force from the pulpit is needed for a
> new church. We had pulpits on the dynamic side in the
> other two congregations we were in. The minister here
> is an organizer, not a preacher."

> "We need a preaching ministry first. If Jesus Christ is
> preached from the pulpit, then you will have a good
> congregation. . . . People come to hear a message."

"Many come to hear [the minister] who don't like his pulpit manners and delivery. [He] is an excellent pastor, warm, of good heart, good for the sick, and good in around-the-room Bible study. We'll have him till he retires. The complainers are usually those who have been in a big city church and had a smooth elocutionist."

"There was a petition to remove the minister, supported particularly by one couple. The wife had been raised a Mennonite and objected to smoking by church members. It is disheartening to see people look critically at a man who has been so beloved. There are complaints that he is not scholarly enough in his sermons, that his voice isn't right, that he deals too much in psychology. He had a quiet, homey style in the small chapel, but that is lost in the large sanctuary. There is no one-to-one relation now; he seems to have lost touch with them."

From the change of heart that appears in these comments, it appears that the minister may become a scapegoat for many of the disappointments that the members feel. Rather than take seriously the possibility of a change of orientation in the congregation, some persons are more inclined to think that a change of ministers would be a solution. The forays, however mild, of the members against the minister, raise the question of how effective he can be in overcoming the inertia of his congregation and bringing about unity on a new tack.

His role is still a difficult one in the developed congregation. The growth of the membership brings new problems to replace old ones. Although less time may be required for the organization of the congregation, there are the continuing jobs of training teachers (a constant difficulty), maintaining leadership for the programs, overseeing the government, and serving the ecclesiastical functions. There are increased demands for counseling services (one of the ministers said he could use a half dozen full-time counselors to handle family problems in his congregation) and additional responsibilities in the community and in the denominational bureaucracy. Because of the indebtedness of the congregation, it is usually impossible to hire additional professional staff, even after the building is up, and many congregations that have reached a respectable size are still serviced by one minister who is hopelessly inundated with demands for his time.

The combined effect of the factors discussed here—the loss of enthusiasm, the emergence of conflict, and the dissatisfaction with the minister—is to inhibit any attempts to bring about broad changes in the thinking of the congregation. It may be that the entrance of a new minister would be a source of enthusiasm, would cancel any obligations the pastor might have to particular factions, and would remove at least temporarily the dissatisfaction the members feel. If so, a change of orientation could at least be considered. However, even with a new minister there are conditions in the congregation which create great pressure for the maintenance of the *status quo*. It is to these conditions that we now turn our attention.

7

STABILIZATION AROUND SURVIVAL GOALS

The need to find a means of resolving conflict among the members is one of the most important tasks of the developed congregation. Furthermore, it must take its resolution without the dramatic visible progress and the wide range of possibilities that were available to the developing congregation. Once the congregation is developed, it already has an established tradition and commitments to honor, and the nature of the survival goals has changed. Nevertheless, the congregation is stalemated in its efforts to effect a significant change in its orientation. Because of this stalemate and pressures for the maintenance of the congregation's organization, it essentially continues its service of the survival goals.

The fact that the developed congregation differs considerably from the developing congregation means, among other things, that there must be some new definition of survival goals. The physical plant now up, a large enough membership attracted, and financial resources found, the congregation's survival depends on somewhat different emphases. Instead of membership recruitment, there is now a greater concentration on maintaining members. Routine efforts to contact new people are carried out, but the well-being of the congregation depends largely on keeping the members it has. Instead of raising a physical plant, there is now the necessity of operating the program that utilizes it. This involves the furnishing of equipment, the insurance of leadership, and the coordination of activities. Instead of raising money to get a building started, the congregation must now raise money to finance its program and reduce its indebtedness.

Although the survival tasks of the developed congregation are not so dramatic as they were at an earlier stage (such as frantically raising several thousand dollars from sixty people in ten days to purchase a good piece of land), they are certainly no easier. In fact, the lack of drama is one reason for the difficulties that are encountered. The developed congregation has to maintain a membership the largest portion of which did not participate in the earliest struggles to organize the church, and thus does not share the *esprit* of the earlier members. Further, there are by now alternatives in the community that compete with the church as an instrument for making social acquaintances; and there are new church groups that are in direct competition with the congregation. There is no longer a rapid population growth, but only a slow turnover. The difficulties of maintaining the interest of the membership is obvious.

The fact that so many of the members are only segmental participants is a special problem for the congregation. Those members who were involved in the organization of the congregation were at least able to gain a broad interest in the shape it was taking. However, the later members have not had an opportunity to be drawn out of their limited interests and thus have only a tenuous loyalty to it. Because of this limited loyalty, it is especially important that a program of diverse interest groups be operated to retain as many of these segmental participants as possible. A look at a list of activities of a developed congregation reveals several dozen regular ones and dozens more special programs. Since many of the activities such as the church school require a great deal of preparation and staffing, one of the congregation's main problems is finding workers to lead them.

"There is a lack of willingness to sacrifice to do a job at times. They say they will and then don't. People are let down. . . . Those who will take jobs have two or three of them. Probably this overloading is a means of discouraging some."

Even those who feel they should be working toward the broader formal goals of the congregation get entangled in the routine chores of the program.

"We don't have enough time to go to meetings of the School Board, or the County Planning Board, etc. We don't infiltrate. We should make our feelings known, for example, to the City Council. There are too many church meetings. In a case of conflict you feel you have to go to the church meetings. The whole community should always be our No. 1 point. We can't continue to grind our wheels in church. . . . I have a picture of the church like a sunburst, going out rather than coming in. . . . One problem of the Presbyterians is that they have too many meetings to discuss meetings."

Nor are the problems connected with the raising of the budget diminished. While there may be more members than there were when the building program was under way, it is no easier to collect the necessary moneys. In fact, the opinion of some of those connected with finances is that it is more difficult.

"Even during the building we had to play it down somewhat. People were subscribing more to it than to the ongoing program. We were ordered in the Every Member Canvass to play down the building program."

"Perhaps people are too much willing to give to a building fund rather than to the operating budget. We try to give one third to missions. I favor it. It's difficult to get people to support the operating budget, but easy to get money for building."

Whatever the difficulties may be in getting the money for the operating budget, there is no way to avoid it.

"Our goals haven't changed much. We still emphasize our own property and needs. We're forced to pay our bills; we've no choice."

These are the survival goals that the congregation now turns its efforts to. Again, it should be pointed out that many of the statements quoted here indicate a dissatisfaction with this situation. However, they are also, for the most part, devoid of much hope that it can be changed. Apparently, the emphasis of the developing congregation on survival goals has consequences that make a later reorientation very difficult. The task of the rest of this chapter will be to examine these consequences and to describe the character of the congregation that results from them.

Morale: Decline of the Dramatic

It has already been pointed out that a large number of the developed congregation's members are segmental participants, and that they did not share in the early tasks of the organization. As segmental participants, they have a limited interest in the congregation and are more concerned with its survival, and thus the satisfaction of their own interest, than with its accomplishment of its formal goals. One of the most dramatic indicators of this condition is seen in relation to the church school, perhaps the congregation's single most ambitious effort. Not only do many persons attend the congregation because of the church school, a number of them also feel an obligation to help with it. But their interest can be rather limited in several ways.

"My children are grown up now, so I don't want anything to do with church school. We go where our interests are."

"Our own church school is in a predicament. Many teachers don't attend church and they talk about not having to. They teach church school but don't use the recommended [official denominational] curriculum. They seem to teach their own credo and prejudices to fill their own needs. The young church school teachers are not related to the ongoing work of the congregation. They are almost in a contest with other groups."

"I've just been going there and teaching because I feel I should. I haven't attended services for the last couple of months."

The weight of this kind of segmental participation is mainly to continue the congregation's program as it is. The interest in change is minimal.

There are two conditions that restrict the introduction of these members to a broader view of the formal goals. First, there is no dramatic need such as was present in the developing congregation to shift their loyalty toward an encompassing of the whole congregation. Second, the segmental participants are not pressed into leadership positions which might well force them to consider the formal goals of the congregation, because these positions are already filled by the members with greater seniority. As a result, their interests remain limited, though they may be shifting. And the program of the congregation must continue to be varied enough to satisfy them.

Another factor that could draw members into wider concern for the congregation, the presence of intimate associations, is also inhibited by the very size of the congregations. There is a spirit of comradery among the older members, but there is little evidence that many of the newer members have been drawn into it. Indeed, even the leaders, who have a particularly good vantage point, confessed that they did not recognize many of the members of their congregations. With such an atmosphere, it is not easy to create a spirit of loyalty to the congregation as a whole.

The character of the suburb as a place of relatively high mobility also has an effect on the extent to which members are integrated into the congregation. A suburban minister reported that he has talked with many people about their church activity and found that they are not sure how long they will be staying in the area, and therefore don't want to get highly involved and have to move away. So the member selects whatever activity suits him, becomes a participant, avoids leadership responsibility, and helps to support the congregation for limited reasons rather than for its formal goals.

The integration of the developed congregation is thus of two kinds. There are the older members, at least some of whom have a loyalty to the congregation as a whole and a vision of the implications of its formal goals; but for the most part they are overworked. And there are the largest part of the members who are loyal to a portion of the program and who must be courted by having their interests served even if they are not the best expression of the formal goals. The need to maintain the support of the members forces the congregation to be solicitous of them, and thus involves them in the continued pursuit of the survival goals.

Authority

There are also features of the authority structure that derive from the developing congregation and make for a continuation of the survival-goal emphasis. In this discussion, we will disregard those pressures from the bureaus of the denomination which might pressure the congregation to try to maintain statistical respectability. Although they may be important, there are conditions internal to the congregations that are equally or more important.

The Minister: Overload. It has already been noted that criticisms of the minister may be instrumental in increasing his insecurity and thus reducing his effectiveness in leading a change in the congregation. However, there is another reason why the minister is unable to devote his full efforts to the reevaluation he so hoped for. He is simply unable to cope with the demands that are made on him by the routine business of the congregation. Most of the men in the developed congregations are working with four hundred to five hundred formal members, plus some constituents who are not members.[55] This is a sizable number for a minister in a small town to serve, but in the suburbs, where there is a constant turnover of membership, it is nearly impossible. Yet the congregations are, for the most part, sufficiently tied up financially that they cannot really consider hiring an assistant minister. The result is that the minister must fill his time with inescapable demands, rely on the lay leaders to keep most of the program going, and neglect the kind of efforts that he would like to make toward reorientation. Where nearly any kind of change in the program would mean training leaders, the minister is forced to bend his efforts to keeping the regular program filled.

In spite of these difficulties, most of the ministers made some effort to provide a new look at the congregation's goals. Changes in the topics of sermons have already been mentioned. One church uses workshops to discuss the minister's sermons. Another runs an intensive religious education program for youth on weekdays after school. These attempts to sharpen education are important and may stimulate change. Several congregations have held weekend retreats at which their goals were discussed: questions of service to society, the nature of the internal life of the congregation, and the obligation of members for individual missions were mentioned. The response to these retreats was that they were "spiritually inspiring," or that members came away with "enthusiasm." However, no specific changes in program were noted. The very crucial job of translating theological imperatives into concrete activities seems to have been the time-consuming, and therefore neglected, one.

Lay Leadership: Entrenchment. There are two ways in which the nature of the lay leadership provides a force for continuing the *status quo*. First, there is an entrenchment of leaders in their positions, so that a rotation that would give a great many people a share in bearing responsibility is difficult. Second, there is a continuation of the influence of the leaders who were early selected for their specialized skills.

The entrenchment of leadership is seen in the assumption by elders that the rotation system means that they will get a year's vacation before being reelected again to their place on the session. Numerous persons said, "This is my year off the session." Although this may mean, on the one hand, that the session members are experienced in their jobs, it may also mean that there is a paucity of new ideas influencing them. And it means that these men who have been responsible for the development of programs will have a stake in the continuation of what they have created. It seems to be very difficult to alter the tendency to entrenchment; all of the congregations reported it. Nor is it only the session that has entrenched leaders. One chairman of a Christian education committee reported that he was currently having trouble because a department church school superintendent wouldn't step down.

The second difficulty, one that is complicated by the first, is that of having men in leadership positions who have been selected for reasons other than their religious maturity. An article some years ago noted that there is a bias in congregations to select leaders who are of some prestigious rank, thus putting a kind of managerial conservatism in control.[56] The same process seems to be at work in the suburban congregations today. One person expressed it in this way:

> "We have forgotten our own obligations in being busy building our own church. We have had professional, educated men on the session. Business men. They have kind of elevated themselves, and treated the church like a big business. But it should be more than that."

Where persons have been put into influential positions to advise on survival goals, it is likely they will continue to emphasize much the same matters, i.e., "practical" concerns. In most of the congregations, it seems there has been this characteristic, and it is one more pressure for considering the survival of the congregation first.

Adaptation to the Parish Area: Increased Competition

The environment presses the congregation toward a survival-goal emphasis in three ways. Two are changes from the conditions of the developing congregation, and one is a continuation.

First, there is a cessation in the growth of the community, together with an increased competition from other religious groups. One congregation, which was the first in its area, now reports ten church buildings within a half mile. Since the commitments of the congregation force it to maintain a certain size membership, it must make an effort to contact new people in the area. Some congregations have an elaborate system for doing this, using members of lay committees. In others, the task falls largely to the minister, adding to his already loaded schedule. The competitive situation further presses the congregation toward maintaining an attractive and varied program to draw potential members.

Second, the community around the congregation is likely to be more established than it was earlier. As a result, there are alternatives of a nonreligious nature for persons who are seeking some kind of social outlet. The establishment of children's organizations such as the Little League and the Scouts involves a lot of parents too, as do branches of fraternal groups and their auxiliaries. Further, there will have been an increase of friendships among residents, and what a person may have sought in formal activities before, he may now find informally. Thus the congregation's program and efforts at recruitment are under competition from another quarter.

Finally, the suburb will still be the clean, healthy, safe, and quiet place it was before. With the growth of children into teen-agers, there is usually an upsurge in juvenile violations of the law, but apart from that, there is little to prick the congregation's social conscience. For many of the congregations, it is not until they are well developed that they have their first funeral service. Nothing short of a conscious and intense effort to relate the suburban congregation to the problems of the larger metropolitan area on which it depends will open for it the possibility of some broader service. It is just this effort that is blocked by the demands of the program oriented to survival.

The Character of the Developed Congregation

The developed congregation for the most part justifies its existence by providing the explicitly religious services related to church school, worship services, and the minister's special offices, such as his leadership at marriages and funerals. The members feel that they are the fitting functions of the church and contribute financially and by participation to these exercises. With a few changes, the character of the developed congregation is very similar to that of the developing congregation.

Community. The developed congregation differs most from the developing congregation in the quality of the internal life that it shows. It has lost the closeness that characterized it at an earlier point. Although the close relationship may exist among some of the original members, it does not permeate the congregation, and even among the older members, there is a feeling of losing touch. The developed congregation is likely to have a sanctuary large enough to seat all of its worshipers at one service. While this is one way of bringing the congregation together, there is the feeling among many that the large number of worshipers reduces the spirit that was present in the smaller services. More strange faces are visible, and visitors tend to pass unrecognized as such. Thus the centering around worship becomes formalized and there is a decline in the community feeling of the congregation. Where it exists at all, it is in small (and rare) groups within the congregations. The emergence of factions supporting different views about how the congregation should proceed are further evidence of the absence of an encompassing community.

Nurture. Church school continues to be emphasized both as a proper concern of the congregation, and to meet the desires of segmental participants. Adult education finds little response in most of the congregations. Where there are small study groups, they are usually enthusiastically supported by their participants, but their size makes it difficult for the minister to justify his spending much time on them. The entrenchment of particular members as a kind of leadership elite reduces some of the opportunity to show individual responsibility for many of the members. The tasks that are constantly available, such as teaching and leading teen-age groups, are too demanding for many of the newer members, and are shunned as too much bother by older members. The popular jobs are those with authority but limited demands, such as the positions as elder, or trustee, or sometimes deacon. Without small and intimate groups there is no way to communicate the activities of the members as individuals in their daily lives. Some members feel this kind of thing is their primary obligation but are constrained by the demands on them for service within the congregation. The attempts to establish small groups in neighborhood areas to foster individual initiative in expressing mission have, for the most part, been weak. There is a lack of laymen who feel competent to lead them, and the minister does not have sufficient time. As a result, the members are inclined to serve within the congregation and rely on denomination agencies or professional staff to put their contributions into effect in the world.

Service. The corporate approach of the congregation to the world is restricted to contacting and recruiting members. Participation in ecumenical services at Thanksgiving, during Lent, and at Christmas is one example of publicity that is not directly aimed at recruitment. However, this kind of approach is nearly nominal. Some congregations allow community groups to use its building for their functions, but this is a rather detached contact. Most of the congregations did not report any attempt to implement their goals for the improvement of society. One had a program of visitation to a home for "elder citizens." Essentially, the congregation in its developed stage has grown into a major operation that requires considerable effort to maintain. It has become more formalized than the developing congregation, and done little more to pursue the full range of its formal goals.

The developed congregation shows no more inclination than did the developing congregation to take risks. Rather, it continues to play it safe so far as its program is concerned. Perhaps more than the developing congregation, it is forced to this condition by its commitments, commitments that were made in its earlier stages.

The early emphasis on survival goals covered misunderstandings and conflicts about the nature of the formal goals, which differences later emerged in crippling disagreements. The selection of early leaders for special talents left the developed congregation with a leadership to some extent unable to deal with a reinterpretation of the formal goals. The design of the program around special interests of segmental members, rather than around the formal goals, forced the congregation to maintain a large and diverse schedule of activities. The early interest in the building committed the congregation to a particular kind of programming (building-centered) and created a heavy indebtedness. The rapid growth of the congregation brought in a large group of unassimilated members who were not particularly interested in the formal goals, but whose presence taxed the energies of the minister and lay leaders.

The result of these developments is a congregation of traditional outline, devoted to its own internal life and with limited prospects of developing a more comprehensive service of its formal goals. It should be kept in mind that within these congregations there are persons who have a broader view of what the congregation should be, i.e., a close fellowship of committed persons making an impact on the world by the quality of their lives. But they are entangled to a large extent in the structures that have developed, and may be more hindered than helped by them.

8

A "DEVIANT" CASE

One of the six congregations in this study was sufficiently different from the other five in the way it developed and in its characteristics to be considered a "deviant" case.[57] (A second congregation was similar to the deviant case in some respects, but it was sufficiently like the norm to warrant its being treated with the majority.) Most of the conditions facing the deviant case were like those facing other congregations, yet it developed a character rather distinctive from the others.

The importance of this case for our analysis should be made explicit. First, by contrast, it clearly demonstrates how there can be different responses to similar conditions. That is, the congregations which are set in similar circumstances are not constrained to respond in the same way. Second, it enables us to look at the *relative efficiency* of the congregations in the light of the formal goals, rather than simply noting that they all fall short of a complete realization of these goals.

The procedure adopted here is to describe first the characteristics of the deviant case in its developed stage, and then examine the manner in which it solved its system problems. In most cases, the contrast with the other congregations will be clear.

The Character of the Deviant Congregation

In the following description of the deviant congregation, its characteristics in the two stages of its development have been combined. The later discussion of the reasons for the difference in this congregation will bring out some of the distinctive traits it had in the developing stage.

Community: Lack of Crises. To some extent, the internal atmosphere of this congregation is very like the others. The original group of members was very close, but the increase in size has sapped much of the vitality of those relationships. Yet the congregation was distinctive in at least one way. This was the only congregation in which none of the respondents could pick out what he would call a "crisis" in its history.

> "I can't think of a crisis. Has anyone else indicated any? 'Crisis' is more serious than applies here. I don't know of any. We've had some pretty good discussions on the session, but it has always come up with a united front afterward."

Nor did anyone feel there were factions within the congregation.

> "There are groupings within the congregation, but not in the sense of being destructive. It's not cliquish in the sense that there are clear sides in a congregational meeting. We get hot discussions within cliques."

Yet even though there are possibly no real divisions within the congregation, there is no clear evidence that there is a positive atmosphere of fellowship in an inclusive sense. Some individual members may feel a part of the congregation in a special sense.

"We built a close fellowship. Now all our friends are there, all of our life is there. I have a deep feeling for my neighbor, a responsibility to be involved for Christian motives. This has developed in association with the church."

But there is at the same time a feeling that there has been a change in the quality of the relationships that are possible, perhaps because of size.

"The bulk of the people have reached a deeper understanding of the church. This is [the minister]. He helps them to a realization. As the church has grown this has become more difficult. [He] can't get to all of them. Working together developed a real sense of fellowship. It's hard to integrate people into the church now. . . . I wonder if the congregation has already lost the koinonia at five hundred members. What will happen at seven hundred?"

There may be a difficulty for any congregation of this size to develop an inclusive fellowship. Probably the main expression of this will be in a core group within the congregation. It appears that this is what has happened in the deviant case. Several small discussion groups evidenced a spirit of closeness, but the body of the congregation is formally associated in the same manner as the other congregations. There is also some evidence that at least some of the members of the congregation know what others are doing in their daily lives to further the church's mission. The communication of this kind of knowledge is itself an indicator of a depth of relationships.

Nurture: "We" Not "They." The congregation has been strong in its intention that it consist in the work of its members and not only in the activities of the professional

clergy. This attitude has been evidenced both in the
chores within the congregation and in the individual expressions of the members outside the church. The participants are aware of this emphasis.

> "This has been more of a layman's organization. That
> was much due to the minister's attitude. 'We' do this,
> not 'they.' "

The emphasis on an awareness of the mission in the lives
of the members can be seen in their activities. They have
been involved in various kinds of service outside of the
congregation such as the National Council of Presbyterian Men, Presbyterial, United Church Women, NAACP,
Mid-Peninsula Citizens Against Proposition 14, Council
of Presbytery, and the Fair Play Council. Most of the
participants hold or held offices in their organizations.
Another striking example is that one of the congregation's
leaders was instrumental in having the Realty Board of
which he is a member become one of the only two in the
state to declare publicly its opposition to Proposition 14.
This is the kind of action that implies a relevance of the
formal goals of the congregation to the whole lives of its
members.

The congregation also intended to limit each member
to one job in the congregation so that responsibility
would be distributed. However, there has been a tendency
for competent members to take on more than one job and
to become entrenched in leadership positions. Perhaps it
is in the congregation's favor that they still attempt to
implement the ideal.

The education program has been greatly emphasized.
The church school is large and has been given priority
over other concerns when there was a question of where
to put funds. And there has been experimentation with,

and a constant program in, adult education. Faculty from nearby seminaries and colleges have been brought in to lead the study groups.

Service: Giving Something Away. The congregation has, like other congregations, turned outward at least to the extent of directing financial support to the agencies of the church, and indeed it has a steadier rate of increase in benevolence giving than other congregations. Its members have attempted to spread the influence of the congregation by becoming involved in numerous community organizations. However, the most impressive evidence of the congregation's service is through its support of a community center in a low-income section of the metropolitan complex in which it is located. This center is located well outside of even the most broadly defined neighborhood of the congregation. The congregation provides financial support for the center, along with two other groups, and contributes to the volunteer staff without which the center could not operate.

The importance of this kind of service for the congregation itself is reflected in the comments of its members about the church.

"The attitude now is one of giving something away. You don't think of that when you're young, but you only get out what you put in."

"The function of the church is to love our neighbor. That means to become involved in politics, and so on, in equal rights and opportunities for all men. The church must be in the people seven days a week, in many places."

"I want to see Christians practice what they preach, for example, on civil rights. They should give a gift of themselves as well as money."

"What you get out is only what you bring in yourself. You have to give something of yourself. My husband and I feel the church is a center from which you go out into the world. It's not just a shell or a self-contained unit. You have to express yourself outside of the church. I remember a television show in which James Baldwin spoke from the burned-out ruin of St. Mary's Cathedral. He said the Negro had called on God and the churches and nothing had happened, so now the Negro is doing the job himself. Most churches are like that dead, empty ruin."

The congregation did not just begin with this orientation; there were evidently times when a different perspective held sway.

"It wasn't until we became aware of [East City] that we, as a congregation, got out of our WASP [white, Anglo-Saxon, Protestant] boundaries. We got out of some of our boundaries and became a servant. . . . We recognized we weren't involved in social life. There was a gradual shift. The Church and Society Committee of the local congregation spent a year educating themselves, then went to the congregation. It's typical of [the minister] that we reach an understanding before we move."

It should be further noted that this kind of attitude is not shared by the entire congregation; there are complaints that most of the members are trying to hide from the world. But the inclination to service was shared by all of the leaders interviewed, and it was reported that the minister can deliver a social-action sermon disagreeable to many and stimulate discussion rather than antagonism.

Sacrifice: Taking a Chance. There are no dramatic acts that point up the congregation's willingness to take risks, but there is a kind of consistent tendency to take other values than survival as a basis for making decisions. For example, the congregation limits the manner in which funds can be raised.

> "The General Assembly said they felt the purpose of the church wasn't to raise funds. So our congregation adopted this and ruled out any fund-raising activities. . . . They even stopped the young people's carnival to raise money to send to other groups. When we decided not to raise money, the congregation said go ahead and do the carnival just for fun. . . . But we need those projects and action programs for this age group. They don't have their own money."

This attitude of running the congregation on the contributions of committed members even affects such typical efforts as the annual canvass of constituents.

> "All members of the session and deacons and wives made friendship calls to the less active members. . . . We presented the program of the church for the coming year to those who had some contact with the church. We didn't ask for pledges, we just presented the program."

There was also an attempt to keep the congregation aimed in the right direction by limiting the kind of programs that could provide special interests which were peripheral to the formal goals. The minister put it this way:

> "The Presbyterian Church spells out its program in breadth. We were afraid of getting too thin. So we asked, 'What is the mission of the church?' And we cut out what does not serve the purpose of the church. We keep only what serves. We cut out potlucks and other strictly social activities. We cut out every kind of money-raising activity. It's only with reluctance that we allow the kids some special thing now. We didn't want ex-

traneous things to become traditional. . . . We gave up
regular meetings for the Men's Chapter; we felt we
should only bring them together for a purpose."

Another of the church leaders commented on the same
matter.

"The Men's Chapter is less well supported. You shouldn't
have an organization for organization's sake. You have
to have a purpose first. This one was otherwise. And you
have to have a good reason for the church. There are so
many activities outside."

Another indication that the congregation did not go directly after survival goals is the fact that though it is the
oldest of the congregations studied, it does not yet have
a sanctuary. It is argued, for example, that young people
want to be married in more plush surroundings, and that
older persons are uncomfortable on folding chairs. All of
the respondents were aware of these arguments.

"[The church], to increase the congregation's size,
should have built a sanctuary early. Some deacons say
the simplicity may have kept some from coming back.
. . . I feel it's what you bring into worship services, not
the surroundings."

The congregation is now in a financial position seriously
to consider building a sanctuary, and indeed plans are in
the drawing-board stage, but the sentiment seems to be
that at present the money is likely to be used to hire an
assistant to the minister to free him for more adult education. Taken together, these bits of evidence suggest that
this congregation at several points has made decisions
for other ends than survival, decisions that are in contrast
with similar ones made by the other congregations considered here.

The main difference between the deviant congregation and the others is that it has realized the full range of its formal goals to a greater extent than they have. The substance of the difference has to do with realizing goals not directly connected with survival. The "deviant" congregation is like the others in its conduct of formal worship, church school, government, recruitment of members, and contributions to the church organization. But it went further and achieved a continuing unity, a germinal sense of community; it emphasized adult as well as children's education, and stimulated and communicated the individual acts of members who expressed their mission in their daily lives; and it sought and found an expression for the corporate entity of the congregation in service to society. Finally, in doing these things, it demonstrated that it was willing to take some risks rather than simply "play it safe." The other congregations may eventually make a transition in the same direction, but at present this congregation is alone in the particular character it developed.

The Development of the Deviant Congregation

With this description of the character of the deviant congregation in mind, we now turn to an investigation of the way the congregation handled its problems. In the course of this discussion, there will also be a description of the conditions that were peculiar to it.

Morale: Single Colony. This congregation differed from others at the start in that it was begun as a single colony of volunteers from a large Presbyterian Church not far away. The earliest members thus had some common background, and were at least interested in the new congre-

gation. Because the former congregation had been so
large, they had not had a great deal of contact with each
other, but they did all know the organizing minister who
had served as an assistant there. This common background may have served the dual function of enhancing
their ability to communicate with each other, and reducing the likelihood of the formation of factions.

The early congregation spent a long while together
before any efforts were made to enlist new members.
There was a concentration on adult study and on leadership training. This may be one reason why the congregation showed the most agreement between the minister
and the members as to what the goals were at the outset.
The period spent together as a somewhat isolated group
also enhanced the group's morale. During this period they
met in rented quarters; even the physical conditions seem
to have contributed to the group's enthusiasm.

> "I can't explain it. It was a wonderful experience. We
> met in a library. Everyone had a job. Even the kids
> would dust off the chairs and things like that. We all
> had responsibility and looked forward to it."

> "Everybody worked like mad. We moved things in and
> out of the library. There are even movies of that time.
> Everyone was willing to do things. This was part of
> everyone's life. This was where we spent our time."

This period gave the members time to get acquainted
without having their attention diverted to other pursuits.

There was a willingness to go slowly about the building. Without the pressure of a rapidly growing membership there was no need to move immediately into the
building. According to the minister:

> "Our main concern was with keeping our benevolence
> giving up as far as finances were concerned. The laymen
> felt that we should go after buildings when they were

necessary, but that they should not become a focus for our attention. There was one fund drive for an education unit. They felt we should concentrate on being the church."

The first education unit was put up by the men themselves and was a source of great cohesion among them, just as similar work had been in the other congregations. However, the growth of the congregation itself never became the primary source of integration. Thus there was little loss of enthusiasm when the survival tasks were completed (although in a sense the lack of a sanctuary could be taken to mean that they have not yet been completed). Persons who felt a change in spirit in the congregation without exception related this to size and the number of new and unknown faces.

The growth of the congregation was slower and steadier than was the case for most of the others. There were no dramatic, sharp rises in membership. This probably enabled the congregation to assimilate members more thoroughly at the start, though at some point the number got beyond the point of adequate assimilation. There were two reasons for the slower rate of membership increase. First, the congregation was organized at the very beginning of the development of the area in which it was to locate. Thus the growth of the population around it was slower. Second, there was no particular effort by the congregation to attract segmental participants. This is indicated by the fact that the program was curtailed so that strictly social activities were out, and by the fact that potential members were probably lost because of the lack of impressive facilities.

The congregation was able to integrate the members without a reliance on survival goals, and this integration was sufficiently related to formal goals to limit the kind of segmental participation that can quickly destroy the congregation's cohesion. That the congregation did not become a closed group is made clear, not only by its eventual size, but also by its interracial composition.

Authority: Security. Sufficient has been said above about the minister as "the man in the middle" to establish that he is subject to great pressures from all sides, and great insecurity as well. The minister of the deviant congregation certainly experienced the same pressures, but his position was much more secure and allowed him a firmer place from which to resist the forces that were counter to the accomplishment of the formal goals.

At the start of the congregation, the minister was serving on the staff of the church from which the first volunteer members came. He had experience in the local presbytery, he was respected by other ministers, he had friends in the area, he was acquainted with the conditions of the environment, and he was just short of having earned a doctorate at a nearby university. He had participated as a staff member in the discussions that led to forming a new congregation and had considerable time to consider the possibilities before he was even approached to take on the job of organizing. As a result, he went into the job with a fairly clear idea of what he wanted to do, and a rather secure position from which to do it. His intention was to orient the congregation from the beginning to its formal goals, and he was willing to take the risks that it might entail.

Because the congregation did not immediately become involved in survival tasks, the leaders were less likely to be selected because of their special skills. Much of the early period of the congregation was given to study and leadership training. Each person had some kind of responsibility, and as the congregation grew, these people would be exercising their responsibility in ways other than those connected directly with building or membership recruitment or fund-raising. Furthermore, there were some members of the early group who had considerable experience in the church and who came to be looked upon as the models of the Christian. There was even the happy circumstance that some of these persons were talented enough to be valuable in the survival tasks.

"John K. is an engineer, a plant manager. His special skills were helpful at the beginning. He is also spiritual; he was the moderator of the presbytery several years ago."

This congregation did not escape the tendency of its leaders to become entrenched in their positions. There have been explicit statements quoted above about this. And the use of the rotation system for elders has not countered the "year off" syndrome. However, there is a possibility that the understanding of the leaders who have become entrenched is somewhat more mature with regard to the formal goals than is true in most of the congregations.

Adaptation to the Parish Area: Gradual Growth. For the most part, the suburban context of the deviant congregation was similar to the others. In two important respects it may be said to differ. First, with regard to the timing, the development of the area around the congregation was steady rather than sudden. Second, the area in which the congregation located is closer to an urban sector than is true of most of the other congregations.

Reference has already been made to the helpful effects of having a slower population growth rate. Something more needs to be said about the second characteristic.

The event that took the congregation outside its "WASP boundaries" was the discovery of conditions in another sector of the urban complex in which it is located. Although this area is considerably outside the congregation's neighborhood, it is still not so far removed as to make travel to it bothersome. Quite possibly, the discovery of this means of service was an important factor in enabling the deviant congregation to maintain its orientation. However, it must not be forgotten that it was as a result of the work of the Church and Society Committee that this outlet was found, and that the work of that committee was impelled by the congregation's understanding of its formal goals.

The main program that the congregation had which was of segmental interest to the community was the church school. This program was probably the source of many persons who became members with only peripheral interest in the congregation. However, the congregation made no special effort to interest such persons, and yet was able to attract a large membership. Part of this was due, especially at the outset, to the comity arrangement under which it had a franchise to organize in that area. Yet even after ten more congregations were established in the area, the congregation has been able to maintain its membership, and continues to grow. It seems clear that a congregation is able to maintain itself without special appeals to segmental participants.

It is also possible that there have been new residents who were looking particularly for a congregation which was attempting to express its formal goals. And these persons would be attracted to the congregation precisely because it is not so involved in peripheral programs. At least one of the leaders who were interviewed stated that this was true for him.

What, in summary, can we say are the reasons the deviant congregation developed as it did? First, the congregation was formed from a single colony of volunteers. As a result, communications within the group were facilitated, and the likelihood of the formation of factions was reduced. This made possible an intense discussion of the formal goals and the eventual achievement of an agreement as to how they should be implemented.

Second, the leadership of the congregation was both inclined and competent to move the congregation toward an expression of the formal goals. The minister not only had an idea of how the congregation should develop, but also felt secure enough to resist such pressures as could divert the congregation toward an emphasis on survival goals. And among the laymen in the earliest group were experienced persons who were already active as individuals in pursuing the church's formal goals. These persons were able to serve as models for the rest of the members and thus give concrete references for the meaning of the formal goals.

Third, the slow rate of population growth in the area, and the emphasis on study and leadership training in the congregation, combined to give the group opportunity to form a character before it began to take in new members. This meant that the basis of enthusiasm in the congregation was other than the survival tasks. The enthusiasm that surrounded the building of the educational units later was an addition to the earlier enthusiasm, and the completion of the building did not cause a radical drop in morale.

Fourth, the conscious decision at an early stage to de-emphasize the building and such social activities as were designed to attract members became a clear sign of the priority that the congregation put on formal goals. The effect of the decision was probably to discourage segmental participants.

Fifth, the location of an expression of the congregation's service goal not only advanced its realization of its formal mission, but also became a constant and concrete reminder to the congregation of its responsibility in this direction. The conscious attempt to locate such a means of service was a result of the intention of the congregation as a whole, and is evidence of the desire to express the formal goals.

The key to the development of the deviant congregation is its attack on the vagueness of the formal goals. This attack was carried out first by study and later by the orientation of concrete decisions around the results of the study. In this process, the character of the earliest stage of the congregation is crucial because the decisions which it makes shape the subsequent program, and the members who later affiliate with the congregation are self-selected to some extent on the basis of the program's shape.

Formal Goals vs. Survival Goals

The contrast between the deviant congregation and the others enables us to draw several conclusions. First, it is not necessary for a congregation to limit itself to an emphasis on survival goals in order to survive. Even when statistical criteria are employed, the record of the deviant congregation is among the best in all categories. It is a case where survival accompanied a dedication to formal goals.

Second, the very real pressures inherent in the conditions under which the new suburban congregation develops, which incline it toward a concentration on survival goals, can be resisted. It is not true that the suburban context necessarily shapes the congregation.

Third, it appears that the ability to resist pressures toward an emphasis on survival goals depends upon the nature of the earliest group of members. On the one hand, a single colony of members is better able to communicate and is less likely to break into contending factions. On the other hand, the leadership should be composed of a relatively secure minister and some laymen who are sufficiently dedicated to serve as concrete referents for the rest of the members.

Finally, it appears that once a congregation has adopted an emphasis on survival goals, it is likely to continue in that emphasis. The argument that once the survival tasks are completed it can turn to its real job does not receive empirical support from this study. The deviant case came closer than the others to realizing its formal goals by running the risk of failing to survive; the others consumed the largest part of their energies in doing battle with that possibility.

9

SUMMARY AND CONCLUSIONS

What remains to be done is to put aside the concrete data which have provided the basis for this analysis, and to state in general terms what has been learned from the study. This will be done in two steps: first a summary of the main findings, and then a statement of some theoretical propositions that seem to follow from these findings.

General Summary

The formal goals of the congregation are stated in symbols that are either vague in meaning or have several meanings. In a new congregation, the diversity of backgrounds represented by the members makes the process of interpreting these formal goals particularly difficult. Often there is a lack of concrete referents, either in persons or activities, by which to give a visible meaning to the formal goals. As a result, there is difficulty in obtaining a consensus in the new congregation on an interpretation of the goals.

Because of the difficulty in interpreting the formal goals, and as a result of other conditions of the new congregation, there is a tendency to give a priority to survival goals. As far as the members are concerned, the survival goals are clear and obviously necessary, and there is a real satisfaction from being able to see progress toward their realization. Furthermore, the suburbs offer highly available resources that can be utilized in the pursuit of the survival goals—potential members, available money, and access to land and construction facilities.

There are also the expectations of the bureaus and agencies, both denominational and those concerned with comity arrangements, which are likely to be expressed in terms associated with the survival goals. The minister, especially, because he is in a position of great insecurity, is likely to feel the pressures very strongly and be tempted to pursue the course that is most likely to give visible evidence of success.

The argument that the accomplishment of the formal goals is dependent upon the accomplishment of the survival goals serves as a satisfactory justification both for the minister and for the members for deferring a complete consideration of the implications of the formal goals. This justification is supported by the vague statements of the formal goals which allows the survival tasks to be considered a nearly adequate fulfillment of the goals.

The early emphasis on survival goals, however, has consequences that make it difficult to alter the congregation's orientation at a later stage. The enthusiastic recruitment of new members results in the gathering of a large number of segmental participants, and the rapid growth makes it impossible to assimilate adequately all the members. The commitments, both financial and in participation, to the buildings, equipment, and program soon force the more active members to direct their energies to maintenance functions.

In addition, the emphasis on survival goals tends to put into positions of authority persons who became prominent by means of their status in the larger community and by utilizing the special skills they bring to further these goals. The leadership is thus less competent than it should be in understanding the congregation's formal goals. Further, these leaders tend to become entrenched in their positions, largely because of their seniority, and thus inhibit further change. The demands on the minister to service a rapidly expanded and relatively unassimilated membership prevent him from devoting his energies to the reorientation of the congregation.

Thus, the vagueness of the formal goals, and pressures to get beyond this vagueness as quickly as possible, lead the congregations toward giving priority to survival goals. And the very success in achieving the survival goals blocks attempts at a later reassessment of the congregation's formal goals. The decisions of the developing congregation are crucial for the character of the developed congregation.

It should be recognized that this summary is a collection of empirical generalizations drawn from only six congregations. As generalizations, they necessarily mask the many variations and details that are part of the concrete cases.

Theoretical Conclusions

In the broad scheme of sociological theory about organizations and institutions, this is a case study of the tendency of organizations to abandon their formal goals and to pursue a course that insures their own survival. It does not purport to challenge or significantly elaborate on the theoretical conclusions of the others who have studied this tendency. However, it may be helpful to state explicitly some theoretical propositions that can be derived from the analysis that was employed here. As the final step in this report, the empirical generalizations made above can be distilled into theoretical propositions which have relevance for organizations operating under the same general conditions as the congregations here studied.

The propositions that are presented here are relevant to organizations which have two characteristics: First, they must be in a state of formulating a program either as a result of a disruption of the usual program or because they are in the process of first organizing. Second, the organization's formal goals must be stated in general enough terms that they are susceptible to a variety of interpretations. It may well be that these propositions can also be relevant to an organization which, while its formal goals are rather clearly defined, has difficulty in achieving them.

The propositions have to do with three kinds of conditions within the organization. There are propositions about the "causes" of an emphasis on survival goals, that is, the functions that an orientation around survival goals fulfills for the organization. There are propositions about the "consequences" of a survival-goal emphasis for the organization. And finally, there are propositions about the kinds of conditions that are necessary to avoid giving survival goals priority over formal goals. The first two sets of statements are derived from the nature of the five congregations that adopted survival-goal emphases. The third set is informed by the deviant case.

The Functions of Survival-Goal Priority. This study has been organized in part around the system problems which organizations must solve in order to retain their structure. There are usually alternative solutions to the problems available to any particular organization. The case that has been made in this paper is that survival goals serve admirably as at least limited solutions to a number of problems that the new congregation faces. As a result, it is possible to summarize our conclusions about the causes for emphasizing survival goals in terms of the system problems.

The possibility of giving survival goals priority over formal goals derives from the vagueness with which the formal goals are stated. As a result, one of the necessary first steps in organizing a congregation is the translation of the formal goals into concrete terms. However, this process is made difficult by the diversity of backgrounds which members bring to the task. This diversity usually leads to conflict about the interpretation of the goals. Thus the reduction of conflict becomes a primary consideration of the organization, and the survival goals are available to serve as a temporary expedient for deferring conflict, and as a reasonable program for future activity:

1. *Where formal goals are difficult to define, there is a tendency to adopt an orientation around survival goals as a means to defer or resolve conflict about the interpretation of formal goals.*

Not only are the survival goals helpful in deferring conflict, they also provide a way to stimulate the incentive of the members. If the translation of the formal goals is blocked, the survival goals can serve as indicators of progress or accomplishment in the organization. The visibility of the fruits of effort put into survival goals increases the enthusiasm of the members, and provides them with specific means by which they can express their enthusiasm:

2. *Where formal goals are difficult to define, there will be a tendency to adopt an orientation around survival goals as a means of focusing attention on concrete, limited tasks, the exercise and completion of which serve to increase morale.*

These two propositions are directly related to the way in which the organization can use survival goals to solve the problems of integration. The survival goals can also help to solve the problems of authority, or pattern maintenance, both within the organization and in relation to such bureaucratic hierarchies as affect its operations.

Where the formal goals are not clearly defined, there is no clear standard by which to evaluate the persons who are to fill leadership positions. In this situation there is an inclination for members to evaluate their potential leaders in terms of their competence in dealing with the concrete, technical tasks that are related to the survival goals. Thus the survival goals become central to the organization, both as a criterion for selecting leaders and as the primary competence of the leaders themselves. The survival goals give shape to the authority structure:

3. *Where formal goals are difficult to define, there will be a tendency to adopt an orientation around survival goals as a means of deriving criteria for the selection and evaluation of leaders.*

Furthermore, if the local congregation is a part of a larger bureaucracy, it will have further reason to look to survival goals to replace vague formal ones. The fact that bureaucracies usually adopt quick and summary means to evaluate the work of the local organization is a strong pressure for the group to adopt an emphasis on survival goals as a means of satisfying the bureaucracy. A new

group particularly may be inclined to accept the bureaucracy's standard of evaluation and try to justify its efforts
according to that standard:

> 4. *Where formal goals are difficult to define, there will
>   be a tendency to adopt an orientation around survival
>   goals as a means of justifying the activities of the
>   local organization to the bureaucracy to which it is
>   responsible.*

The organization that is operating with vague formal
goals is likely to encounter difficulty in clarifying to its
"clientele" the nature of the service that it intends to
render. In this situation, it will be inclined to recognize
and emphasize those activities which secure the most
response from the environment. This process of shaping
activities to secure response, part of which is in terms of
resources, is in effect a process of elevating survival above
formal goals. Thus the organization adapts so effectively
to its environment that it becomes dependent upon the
environment to validate the organization's operations:

> 5. *Where formal goals are vaguely defined, there will
>   be a tendency to adopt an orientation to those activi-
>   ties which secure the greatest response from the en-
>   vironment and thus validate the organization's exis-
>   tence, and which provide resources necessary for the
>   organization's survival.*

These are the ways in which the organization with
vague goals can feel a strong attraction to an orientation
around survival goals. A few of them may be relevant for
any particular organization, but once the step is made
toward giving priority to survival goals, the rest will give
added impetus to the organization's movement in that
direction.

The Consequences of Survival-Goal Priority. As was indicated by the two stages of the development of new congregations, there are changes in the kinds of tasks that are related to survival goals. We can distinguish at least the earliest efforts to accumulate the resources and participants that make up the organization, and the later efforts to maintain them. In part, this change in tasks is anticipated by the organization and the intention is that a reevaluation will take place when the change occurs. However, the changes in tasks are accompanied by a loss of morale that seriously impairs any attempt at reorientation. Even though there are survival tasks to be carried out in the developed organization, they do not have the dramatic flavor that the earliest tasks had.

Two of the functions that the early survival tasks served for the organization are continued. The bureaucracy still makes its evaluations in terms of criteria related to the survival goals, and the response of the environment is still taken to be a measure of the validity of the work of the organization. However, the other functions related to the internal life of the organization are not fulfilled by the later, more mundane, survival tasks. The result is a loss of morale and the carrying out of tasks because of obligation rather than from enthusiasm.

The early survival tasks had been dramatic enough, and pressing enough, to divert the attention of the members from real differences of understanding among them. This diversion was important for the integration of the early group. However, the evidence is that in the interim, the differences have not been reconciled, but rather break out anew when the diversion is gone. The conflicts in the developed organization are at least as serious as they were at an earlier stage because the disputants now feel that they have a right to their opinions because of the contributions they have made to the organization. Thus the survival goals can be functional for integration at one point and dysfunctional at a later point:

6. *Where an organization has oriented itself around survival goals, there will be a tendency for conflict to emerge in the organization when there is a change in the nature of the survival goals.*

A similar problem emerges, with the change in survival tasks, that has direct bearing on the morale of the organization. Where the orientation has been to survival goals, and where these goals have been sought through dramatic tasks, there is a sharp loss of enthusiasm with the routinization of the survival tasks. There is a feeling both of having earned a respite from intense participation because of the member's contributions to the early tasks, and a disappointment that the results are less dramatic than the efforts themselves were. The element of anticipation that was present in the earlier tasks is severely tempered in the later tasks and is evident in the loss of incentive:

7. *Where an organization has oriented itself around survival goals, there will be a tendency for a decline in enthusiasm when there is a change in the nature of the survival goals.*

The change in the survival tasks also affects the evaluation of the organization's leaders. The earlier tasks have provided standards that are no longer applicable. The persons who were so competent when the tasks were dramatic may appear less appealing when operations become more routine. Thus there can be a dissatisfaction with the leaders brought about by the very criteria by which the leaders were first selected. A change in conditions can be dysfunctional for the organization by bringing its leaders into disrepute:

8. *Where an organization has oriented itself around survival goals, there will be a tendency for dissatisfaction with the leadership when there is a change in the nature of the survival goals.*

In these ways, an early emphasis on survival goals can eventuate in a loss of integration among the members. Not only is this loss a problem for the routine operations of the organization; it also makes any attempt to reorient the organization very difficult.

Alternatives to Survival-Goal Priority. The main condition for the development of an orientation around survival goals is the vagueness with which the formal goals are stated. It follows then that the essential process for establishing a proper orientation around formal goals is the translation of the formal goals into concrete tasks which are appropriate for the specific organization. It then becomes important to know what kinds of conditions would enhance this process of translation. On the basis of differences between the deviant congregation and the others, it is possible to make some suggestions about what these conditions might be.

One of the conditions that creates pressure for giving priority to survival goals is the presence of conflict in the organization. This conflict is in large part a result of the diversity of understandings that are represented in the earliest members. Thus one way to reduce conflict is to reduce the diversity of understandings that are repre-

sented in the developing organization until an agreement
on its orientation is reached. In terms of new church
development, this means that the single-colony approach
is probably superior to others because it brings together
members with similar backgrounds (with the one condition that the similarity not consist in an emphasis on
survival goals). This similarity provides a basis for communication and a sense of common intention which allows for a more thorough discussion of the formal goals:

9. *The possibility of orienting an organization around
   formal goals is enhanced where the diversity of understandings of the earliest members is minimized.*

Closely related to the preceding condition, is the necessity of having sufficient time to consider the formal goals
in depth. The pressure for a rapid organization reduces
the amount of time that can be given to translating the
formal goals and tempts the organization to begin immediately on survival tasks. The length of time available to
consider the formal goals is partly a result of the speed of
development of the area in which the congregation will
be located, and partly a result of bureaucratic pressures.
If this condition is to be fulfilled, it means that the establishment of a new organization must be begun well ahead
of the time when it is expected to be giving full expression
to its formal goals. If sufficient time is allowed for study
of the formal goals, there can be a sufficiently comprehensive translation of them into concrete terms to indicate
clearly the organization's intentions:

10. *The possibility of orienting an organization around
    formal goals is enhanced where sufficient time is al-
    lowed for the translation of the goals into concrete
    terms before the organization is expected to begin
    operations to realize them.*

The key personnel in the new congregation are the minister and such lay leaders as have grasped the intent of the formal goals and attempt to practice them in their own lives. In the case of the minister, there is great pressure, both from members and from agencies to which he is responsible, to adopt an orientation to survival goals. It is necessary, then, that he be sufficiently secure in his position to be able to make his decisions on the basis of his understanding of the formal goals, rather than to insure the creation of an impression of success. The minister is likely to be more secure if he has some knowledge of the conditions in which he will work and the people with whom he will work, and if his colleagues have other bases on which to evaluate him than his work with the new church alone. It may be that recruiting new church ministers from neighboring churches would be the best way to promote this kind of security:

11. *The possibility of orienting an organization around formal goals is enhanced where the professional leadership is sufficiently secure that they need not establish an image of success by promoting survival goals.*

The lay leadership is also extremely important in the process of translating the formal goals into concrete expression. This translation is considerably expedited where members are able to use the lay leaders as models in understanding the formal goals. The minister is not an appropriate model for the members because he is "paid" for his service; the efforts of lay leaders cannot be so easily dismissed. Thus the presence in a group that is organizing a new church of lay leaders who understand the formal goals and are able to express them is very important in promoting the orientation of the whole group around them:

12. *The possibility of orienting an organization around
formal goals is enhanced where there are some lay
leaders who can serve as concrete models of the expression of the formal goals.*

Finally, the pressures that come from agencies in the
bureaucracy are instrumental in promoting an orientation
to survival goals. While their intentions are stated in terms
of formal goals, the criteria by which they evaluate new
churches are often directly related to survival tasks. Thus
the achievement of formal goals would be promoted by
either a de-emphasis of the survival goals by the agencies
or at least the adoption of a more comprehensive standard. This standard would include a consideration of the
means by which the new churches were attempting to
meet their obligations to the formal goals. Such a change
would relieve the pressure on the ministers and on their
lay boards and would allow for, perhaps force, a more
serious consideration of the formal goals:

13. *The possibility of orienting an organization around
formal goals is enhanced where the bureaucracy to
which the organization is responsible gives clear
evidence that the pursuit of formal goals has a
primary place in its evaluation.*

These propositions are intended to suggest some of the
conditions which contribute to goal subversion. They are,
of course, open to empirical testing and further specifica-
tion. The analysis upon which they are based differs in
several respects from other organizational studies that
touch on the same topic. First, the organization's focus
on survival tasks has been taken to be more than a pre-
occupation with means; it has been conceived of as the
elevation of particular means to the status of goals to the
exclusion of other goals. Second, the analysis has at-

tempted to uncover the dynamics of goal subversion rather than merely to indicate its presence. Finally, the analysis has been concerned with the Protestant congregation as an organization, a concern that limits to some extent the generality of its findings.

The first of the two characteristics of the congregation that sets it apart from other organizations is the vagueness with which its goals are stated. Thompson and Bates point out that the latitude which an organization has in deciding how to implement its goals is directly related to their tangibility, which is defined as "the precision with which the product can be described, the specificity with which it can be identified, and the extent to which it can be measured and evaluated."[58] Obviously, many organizations, such as those in the manufacturing industry, have very tangible goals and thus, for them, goal subversion is possible to a very limited extent. (However, even within manufacturing, there are vagaries in implementing goals, for example, in the allocation of resources to research and development.) It can be speculated that there are instances in which organizations with highly tangible goals may have difficulty in achieving them, and resort to an emphasis on survival in the hope of eventually overcoming these difficulties.

A second characteristic that distinguishes the congregation is the difference between formal and survival goals. It is possible for the survival goals to be pursued while the formal goals are to some extent neglected. This condition has serious implications for the voluntary association. It means that the functions of integration of members, legitimation of authority, and adaptation to the environment, can be accomplished on grounds other than the service of the full range of formal goals. When the orientation of the organization is the service of only a segment of the formal goals, or some entirely secondary activity, it can be called spurious.

However, organizations differ in the extent to which survival goals and formal goals can be separated. Where they are nearly identical, as in most rationally ordered, economic organizations, we are postulating that the possibility of goal subversion is radically reduced. In this case, survival is itself an indication of "success" in terms of the formal goals.

These characteristics of organizations, the degree of tangibility of goals, and the degree to which survival and formal goals are identical, determine the possibility of goal subversion. The character of the Protestant congregation is such that it has a great potential for such subversion. For this reason, the preceding analysis should be seriously considered as relevant not only for new churches but for those already well established.

NOTES

1. Among the sociological papers that have dealt with this process are: Burton R. Clark, *Adult Education in Transition: A Study of Institutional Insecurity* (University of California Press, 1956); M. Greenblatt, R. H. York, and E. L. Brown, *From Custodial to Therapeutic Patient Care in Mental Hospitals* (Russell Sage Foundation, 1955); Paul M. Harrison, *Authority and Power in the Free Church Tradition: A Social Case Study of the American Baptist Convention* (Princeton University Press, 1959); Robert Michels, *Political Parties: A Sociological Study of the Oligarchical Tendencies of Modern Democracy,* tr. by Eden and Cedar Paul (Free Press, 1949); Philip Selznick, *TVA and the Grass Roots: A Study in the Sociology of Formal Organization* (University of California Press, 1949); David L. Sills, *The Volunteers: Means and Ends in a National Organization* (The Free Press of Glencoe, 1957).

2. Peter L. Berger in *The Noise of Solemn Assemblies: Christian Commitment and the Religious Establishment in America* (Doubleday & Company, Inc., 1961) stresses the critical position of the local congregation both for sociological analysis and for theological renewal. Cf. p. 158.

3. H. Paul Douglass and Edmund de S. Brunner, *The Protestant Church as a Social Institution* (Harper & Brothers, 1935). This work includes a consideration of the congregation as a social organization, though the main intent was to deal more broadly with Protestant religion as an institution of American society.

4. Douglass made some move toward a theoretical conceptualization of the congregation as an organization by the comparative work of his book *1000 City Churches: Phases of Adaptation to Urban Environment* (Institute of Social and Religious Research, 1926). The Bureau of Research and Survey of the National Council of Churches has shown interest in the direction of a comparative analysis of survey work in, for example, the 1961 mimeographed paper "Some Recent Research Perspectives on City Church Laity."

5. An example of this approach is Harrison, *op. cit.*

6. See, for example: Bryan Wilson, "An Analysis of Sect Development," *American Sociological Review*, Vol. 24 (1959), pp. 3–15; John M. Yinger, *Religion in the Struggle for Power: A Study in the Sociology of Religion* (Duke University Press, 1946).

7. Among the works in this direction are: Allen W. Eister, "Religious Institutions in Complex Societies," *American Sociological Review*, Vol. 22 (August, 1957), pp. 387–391; Charles Y. Glock, "Religion and the Integration of Society," *Review of Religious Research*, Vol. 2 (Fall, 1960), pp. 49–61; Will Herberg, *Protestant—Catholic—Jew: An Essay in American Religious Sociology* (Doubleday & Company, Inc., 1955); Gerhard Lenski, *The Religious Factor* (Doubleday & Company, Inc., 1961); David O. Moberg, *The Church as a Social Institution* (Prentice-Hall, Inc., 1962).

8. For example, James Swift has found significant differences between congregations in the same denomination in the way leadership is represented. Reported by Charles Y. Glock in "Afterword: A Sociologist Looks at the Parish Church," in Walter Kloetzli, *The City Church, Death or Renewal: A Study of 8 Urban Lutheran Churches* (Muhlenberg Press, 1961), p. 186.

9. Among papers worthy of note as exceptions to the general trends observed here are: Joseph H. Fichter, *Social Relations in the Urban Parish* (The University of Chicago Press, 1954) and *Southern Parish* (The University of Chicago Press, 1951), and Charles Y. Glock, "Afterword: A Sociologist Looks at the Parish Church," in Kloetzli, *op. cit.*

10. A summary of Parsons' formulation of system problems can be found in his paper, "General Theory in Sociology," in

Robert K. Merton, Leonard Broom, and Leonard S. Cottrell, Jr. (eds.), *Sociology Today: Problems and Prospects* (Basic Books, Inc., Publishers, 1959). Parsons here and in his paper, "Suggestions for a Sociological Approach to the Theory of Organizations," *Administrative Science Quarterly*, Vol. 1 (1956), pp. 63–85, 225–239, develops a further scheme of analysis in which four levels of organization can be distinguished in terms of their function for the system as a whole. While helpful in the study of larger organizations, this approach has not been adopted in this paper. Parsons also emphasizes the distinction between the cultural, social, and psychological levels in the study of social systems, but these distinctions are not explicitly made in this paper. Cf. Talcott Parsons and Edward A. Shils (eds.), *Toward a General Theory of Action* (Harper & Row, Publishers, Inc., 1962), especially pp. 53–56.

11. See Philip Selznick, "Foundations of the Theory of Organization," *American Sociological Review*, Vol. 13 (February, 1948), pp. 25–35. In the course of making his main point Selznick notes that the maintenance of the system as a generic need may be specified in terms of certain imperatives. He mentions security with regard to environment, stability of lines of authority and communication, stability of informal relations, continuity of policy, and agreement of meaning of the organization. The first three correspond to Adaptation, Pattern Maintenance, and Integration, the latter two to the area of Goal Attainment. See also the section on "Associations" in Leonard Broom and Philip Selznick, *Sociology* (Row, Peterson & Co., 1956), pp. 203–205 ff.

12. "Two Approaches to Organizational Analysis: A Critique and a Suggestion," *Administrative Science Quarterly*, Vol. 5 (September, 1960), pp. 257–278. Etzioni is begging the question when he suggests as the main query for the "system model," "Under the given conditions, how close does the organizational allocation of resources approach an optimum distribution?" Obviously, the key to this approach is finding the criterion by which to identify the "optimum." Etzioni's interest in this article leads him to neglect the necessity of taking the formal goals of the organization into account in an evaluation. Although it is important not to limit the evaluation

to a comparison of the real social entity with the formal ideal, and although the organization can modify its formal goals and still be of great value, the operation of the organization can nevertheless be evaluated from a perspective outside of the system in terms of its formal goals. In the case treated in this paper, the congregation may be rendering a valuable service in some way, but from the view of the church at large have lost its *raison d'être*.

13. For example, there are no indexed references to religion or to the church in the recent comprehensive review of formal organizations theory in Peter M. Blau and W. Richard Scott, *Formal Organizations: A Comparative Approach* (Chandler Publishing Company, 1962). From his broad perspective of the nation as a social system, Parsons tentatively classifies religious groups as contributing mainly to "pattern maintenance" functions through the creation and continuation of cultural patterns. Groups in this category have much to do with socialization, especially with regard to matters important in the long run rather than the short run: matters calling for the support of "higher" interests and involving self-sacrifice. ("Suggestions for a Sociological Approach to the Theory of Organizations," pp. 229–231.)

14. For example, the congregation fits into both the "mutual benefit" and "service" categories of Blau and Scott's "*cui bono*" typology (*op. cit.*, pp. 43, 45–49, 51–54).

15. James M. Gustafson, "The Clergy in the United States," *Daedalus*, Vol. 92 (Fall, 1963), pp. 724–744, and Samuel Blizzard, "The Minister's Dilemma," *The Christian Century*, Vol. 73 (1956), pp. 508–510.

16. Among the relevant works are: Bennett M. Berger, *Working-Class Suburb* (University of California Press, 1960); Frederick A. Shippey, *Protestantism in Suburban Life* (Abingdon Press, 1964); and Gibson Winter, *The Suburban Captivity of the Churches: An Analysis of Protestant Responsibility in the Expanding Metropolis* (Doubleday & Company, Inc., 1961). The description in this study which is based on the writer's observations agrees rather more with Winter than the rest. Shippey in stressing the possibilities for creative action by the churches in suburbia makes a rather unconvincing

argument that there is a great deal of variation within suburbs, and that life there is very much the same as in small-
town America. Bennett Berger takes the task of arguing
against the inevitable adoption of middle-class culture of the
residents of the suburbs. He bases his case on a study of
working-class persons who had been in a suburb for only two
years. He sees the characteristics of mobility, homogeneity,
and middle-class culture as parts of the "suburban myth," although the persons he was studying had moved there explicitly to retain the jobs they had in a Ford plant that had been
relocated. While it is questionable to explain such findings as
a special case, there are weaknesses in the execution of the
study that render it inconclusive. There is evidence on the
other side that even when special efforts have been made to
induce industry into the suburbs and to construct a balanced
community, the limited price range of available housing has
been a hindrance, and one such venture required workers to
commute from a nearby city. Cf. *Housing and the Future of
Cities in the Bay Area,* by the late Catherine Bauer Wurster.
It is one of the Franklin K. Lane Project papers published by
the Institute of Governmental Studies, University of California Press, 1963. Note especially pp. 30–34.

17. "Religion and the Integration of Society," especially pp.
60–61.

18. "The Norm of the Church," *The Journal of Religious
Thought,* Vol. 4 (1946–1947), pp. 9, 10.

19. H. Richard Niebuhr, in collaboration with Daniel Day
Williams and James M. Gustafson, *The Purpose of the Church
and Its Ministry: Reflections on the Aims of Theological Education* (Harper & Brothers, 1956), p. 31. The generality of the
formulation that Niebuhr adopted is seen further in his definition of love. "By love we mean at least these attitudes and
actions: rejoicing in the presence of the beloved, gratitude,
reverence, and loyalty toward him." (P. 35.)

20. Martin E. Marty, *The New Shape of American Religion*
(Harper & Brothers, 1958), p. 112.

21. P. L. Berger, *op. cit.,* pp. 160 ff.

22. Among the more influential books are: Hendrik Kraemer, *A Theology of the Laity* (The Westminster Press, 1958);

Francis O. Ayres, *The Ministry of the Laity: A Biblical Exposition* (The Westminster Press, 1962); Father Yves Congar, *Lay People in the Church: A Study for a Theology of the Laity* (The Newman Press, 1957); and *Layman's Church,* John A. T. Robinson, *et al.* (Alec E. Allenson, Inc., 1963).

23. Robinson, *et al., op. cit.,* p. 17.

24. Winter, *op. cit.,* pp. 158–159.

25. P. L. Berger, *op. cit.,* pp. 140–157.

26. Winter, *op. cit.,* pp. 71, 140. Italics in the original.

27. H. R. Niebuhr, in *The Purpose of the Church and Its Ministry,* p. 41.

28. Martin E. Marty, *Second Chance for American Protestants* (Harper & Row, Publishers, Inc., 1963), p. 144. In another place in the same connection Marty writes: "The Christian, most of all, can judge, lament, and weep over the world's agonies, its failure to recognize where its own good lies. He can also be free to rejoice in the world's good fortunes. No longer does he view the world from a fortress, from the distance of a sacred place. He is called to go into it, impelled to be its servant. God is to be served and praised not in the fortress but out there in the City of Man" (p. 85).

29. Quoted in Robert McAfee Brown, *The Significance of the Church* (The Westminster Press, 1956), p. 78.

30. Paul Tillich, *The Protestant Era,* tr. by James Luther Adams (The University of Chicago Press, 1948).

31. P. L. Berger, *op. cit.,* pp. 166 ff.

32. Winter, *op. cit.,* p. 36. Winter explicitly criticizes the churches for substituting survival for their proper ministry.

33. Marty, *The New Shape of American Religion,* pp. 130–131. Marty goes on to point out that many readers complained that these churches could not possibly be creative because their memberships were not growing fast enough; these comments in themselves are evidence to support his point.

34. Elizabeth O'Connor, *Call to Commitment* (Harper & Row, Publishers, Inc., 1963).

35. "Of the Admission to Full Communion of Baptized Persons," The Directory for Worship, in *The Constitution of The United Presbyterian Church in the United States of America* (General Assembly of the United Presbyterian Church, 1958),

p. 106. There is an alternative form of this vow which is, however, very similar in substance.

36. The Form of Government, in *ibid.*, pp. 119, 120, 121–122.

37. Selznick has used the term "operational goals" for a similar, though not precisely the same, phenomenon. His concern is with daily operations in a large bureaucracy which do not necessarily affect directly the survival of the organization, as is the case here. He uses "professed goals" in the same sense in which we have used "formal goals," and his comments on the relation of the two are relevant to this discussion. "Running an organization, as a specialized and essential activity, generates problems which have no necessary (and often an opposed) relationship to the professed or 'original' goals of the organization. The day-to-day behavior of the group becomes centered around specific problems and proximate goals which have primarily an internal relevance. Then, since these activities come to consume an increasing proportion of the time and thoughts of the participants, they are—from the point of view of actual behavior—*substituted* for the professed goals." (Italics in the original. Philip Selznick, "An Approach to a Theory of Bureaucracy," *American Sociological Review*, Vol. 8 [February, 1943], p. 48.)

38. The system problems which Parsons proposes as inherent in all social systems is an example of the positing of functional requisites on this analytical level.

39. This vagueness in the definition of the formal goals is one of the chief characteristics of the congregation, and one of the factors that contributes to organizational instability, to what Clark (following Selznick) calls "precarious values." "Social values tend to be precarious when they are undefined. This concerns the link between general value conceptions and a proximate set of goals and norms. Values are undefined when they are not embodied in existing goals and standards of committed groups. They lack specific normative reference and no one knows what various symbols really mean." (Burton R. Clark, "Organizational Adaptation and Precarious Values," *American Sociological Review*, Vol. 21 [1956], pp. 327–336.)

40. A good example of this orientation comes from a re-

spected church leader who has been connected with several new churches. "It's a disservice for a congregation to have a [building that is only partly done]. It's very important for the sanctuary to come first and the Christian education units second. If you have cramped quarters you lose a lot of people, and that hurts just on the business basis of having to pay for the building. Many people would like an established building. You don't get first-class people into a second-class dining room."

41. See the discussion of commitment at the different levels of norms, values, and beliefs, in Charles Y. Glock, "Religion and the Integration of Society," *Review of Religious Research*, Vol. 2, No. 2 (Fall, 1960), especially pp. 51–55.

42. These conflicts can be described as the result of a lack of "institutionalized priorities" in the church, and more particularly in the specific congregations. Since the statements of goals are not in the form of concrete activities, there is no necessary agreement on a standard that can be utilized in making decisions. Cf. Talcott Parsons, *The Social System* (Free Press, 1951), pp. 302–303.

43. This process is called "compartmentalization" by Goode in his theoretical statements on mechanisms for reducing role strain. This discussion is relevant to this paper because role strain is in many respects parallel to goal conflict. Indeed, the internalized goal conflict is the role strain here. Cf. William J. Goode, "A Theory of Role Strain," *American Sociological Review*, Vol. 25 (August, 1960), pp. 483–496.

44. On the interest of new members in religious training, see Dennison Nash and Peter L. Berger, "The Child, the Family, and the 'Religious Revival' in Suburbia," *Journal for the Scientific Study of Religion*, Vol. 2, No. 1 (Fall, 1962), pp. 85–93; and G. Paul Musselman, *The Church on the Urban Frontier* (The Seabury Press, Inc., 1960), p. 45. Whyte considers the desire for community to have been a central impetus of religious interest in the suburbs he studied. William H. Whyte, Jr., *The Organization Man* (Doubleday & Company, Inc., 1957), pp. 421 f.

45. Winter, *op. cit.*, pp. 94–98.

46. This is the process that accompanies the principle,

called "multitudinism" by Martin Thornton, that the local church must somehow touch the maximal number of people in the community through the minimal means. Thornton takes issue with this principle in his book *Pastoral Theology: A Reorientation* (London: S.P.C.K., 1956). Marty deals with this debate in *The New Shape of American Religion*, pp. 134 ff.

47. On this dual pressure, see Glock, "Afterword: A Sociologist Looks at the Parish Church," in Kloetzli, *op. cit.*, pp. 182 f.; and Andrew M. Greeley, *The Church and the Suburbs* (Sheed & Ward, Inc., 1959), p. 63.

48. The discrepancies between the minister's and the parishioners' views of the minister's work are well stated in Charles Y. Glock and Philip Roos, "Parishioners' Views of How Ministers Spend Their Time," *Review of Religious Research*, Vol. 2 (Spring, 1961), pp. 170–175. Cf. also Blizzard, *loc. cit.*

49. Dr. John Chandler, who has been a new-church pastor and has written on the subject, and who now works with a New Church Development board, claims that the rate of psychological breakdowns and demitting of the ministry is much higher among new-church ministers than men in other types of pastorates. His opinion has been seconded by a number of other new-church workers.

50. Selznick points to the danger of even temporary capitulation by the organizational leader: "The default of leadership shows itself in an acute form when organizational achievement or survival is confounded with institutional success. To be sure, no institutional leader can avoid concern for the minimum conditions of continued organizational existence. But he fails if he permits sheer organizational achievement, in resources, stability, or reputation, to become the criterion of his success. A university led by administrators without a clear sense of values to be achieved may fail dismally while steadily growing larger and more secure." Philip Selznick, *Leadership in Administration: A Sociological Interpretation* (Row, Peterson & Co., 1957), p. 27.

51. A quotation by Wesley C. Baker, who has ministered to new congregations, is relevant here: "To meet the stipulated requirements of having a local board of elders, we picked the

six most worthy, however untrained, people in the congregation to be the first such officers" (*The Split-Level Fellowship*
[The Westminster Press, 1965], p. 71).

52. In the manual given to new-church pastors for guidance, the suggestion is made that about two months be
allowed for prospect-calling and organizational-promotion,
and another three to six months for worship services and other
steps before the actual organization of the church. While the
manual stresses the need for adequate training and study before organization, the interpretation of this suggestion in the
specific cases is made by regional agencies. Richard S. Mc-
Carroll, *A Guide for the Development of a New Church*
(Board of National Missions, The United Presbyterian
Church U.S.A., 1960), Ch. VI, pp. 3–4.

53. Bennett Berger in his study found little change with
regard to religion in the persons who had been two years out
of the city and in the suburbs. For those whose activity did
increase, he hypothesized, "What it apparently does provide,
at least to the Baptists, is the partial recapture of the solidarity of their rural past; but it is a new kind of solidarity,
rooted not in rural poverty but in suburban domestic com-
fort" (*op. cit.*, p. 53). The search for community that Berger
mentions is supportive of the thesis above; the limited search
is probably due to the working-class sample he was studying.

54. Clark points out in his study of adult education in Los
Angeles that leaders of the program eventually adopted an
ideology of "service" defined by consumer preference, in contrast to a creative attempt to retain some orientation of formal
goals. The goals of the operation then become a response to
the demands of the public rather than from the formal goals.
(Burton R. Clark, *op. cit.*, pp. 145 ff.) In the case of the new
church, a similar charge may be laid on the minister who,
partially because of his being heir to too many demands,
acquiesces to the desires of the bulk of his parishioners.

55. The new-church development manual makes this statement: "Viewpoints as to the ideal size for a church vary greatly
among consultants, areas, and situations, from 400 to 600,
600 to 800, or 800 to 1000. Adjustments are made downward
to 200 to 300 members or even less for isolated localities and

communities of limited growth, or for specialized ministries where a church is needed, regardless of the potential for membership and self-support. Generally, a membership in the vicinity of 500 is about all one minister should attempt to handle, while a membership near the 1000 mark, or even up to 1500, provides the possibilities for adequately supporting a multiple staff of specialists." McCarroll, *op. cit.*, Ch. IV, E, 4. The recommendation is not clear on what happens between 500 and 1000 members, but more important, it does not explicitly recognize the difference in what is required of a minister in a mobile suburban area from what would be required in a small-town church.

56. Jerome Davis, "The Social Action Pattern of the Protestant Religious Leader," *American Sociological Review*, Vol. 1 (February, 1936), pp. 105–144.

57. "Deviant" is used here solely in the sense of differing from the general pattern. No value judgment should be inferred as a result of the way the term may be employed in other sociological studies.

58. James D. Thompson and Frederick L. Bates, "Technology, Organization, and Administration," *Administrative Science Quarterly*, Vol. 2 (December, 1957), p. 329. The authors consider the adaptability of the technology, and the ratio of mechanization to professionalization of the technology, as other important variables in policy decisions. These variables may not be wholly irrelevant to an analysis of the congregation, but the scope of this study precludes giving attention to them here.

BIBLIOGRAPHY

Ayres, Francis O., *The Ministry of the Laity: A Biblical Exposition* (The Westminster Press, 1962).

Baker, Wesley C., *The Split-Level Fellowship* (The Westminster Press, 1965).

Berger, Bennett M., *Working-Class Suburb* (University of California Press, 1960).

Berger, Peter L., *The Noise of Solemn Assemblies: Christian Commitment and the Religious Establishment in America* (Doubleday & Company, Inc., 1961).

Bigman, Stanley K., "Evaluating the Effectiveness of Religious Programs," *Review of Religious Research,* Vol. 2 (Winter, 1961), pp. 97–121.

Blau, Peter M., and Scott, W. Richard, *Formal Organizations: A Comparative Approach* (Chandler Publishing Company, 1962).

Blizzard, Samuel, "The Minister's Dilemma," *The Christian Century,* Vol. 73 (1956), pp. 508–510.

Broom, Leonard, and Selznick, Philip, *Sociology* (Row, Peterson & Co., 1956).

Brown, Robert McAfee, *The Significance of the Church* (The Westminster Press, 1956).

Clark, Burton R., *Adult Education in Transition: A Study of Institutional Insecurity* (University of California Press, 1956).

——— "Organizational Adaptation and Precarious Values," *American Sociological Review,* Vol. 21 (1956), pp. 327–336.

Congar, Father Yves, *Lay People in the Church: A Study for a Theology of the Laity* (The Newman Press, 1957).

Constitution of The United Presbyterian Church in the United States of America (Office of the General Assembly of The United Presbyterian Church in the U.S.A., 1958).

Davis, Jerome, "The Social Action Pattern of the Protestant Religious Leader," *American Sociological Review,* Vol. 1 (February, 1936), pp. 105–144.

Donovan, John D., "The Social Structure of the Parish," in C. J. Nuesse and T. J. Harte (eds.), *Sociology of the Parish* (Bruce Publishing Company, 1951).

Douglass, H. Paul, and Brunner, Edmund de S., *The Protestant Church as a Social Institution* (Harper & Brothers, 1935).

Douglass, H. Paul, *1000 City Churches: Phases of Adaptation to Urban Environment* (Institute of Social and Religious Research, 1926).

Eister, Allen W., "Religious Institutions in Complex Societies," *American Sociological Review,* Vol. 22 (August, 1957), pp. 387–391.

Etzioni, Amitai, "Two Approaches to Organizational Analysis: A Critique and a Suggestion," *Administrative Science Quarterly,* Vol. 5 (September, 1960), pp. 257–278.

Fichter, Joseph H., *Social Relations in the Urban Parish* (The University of Chicago Press, 1954).

―――― *Southern Parish* (The University of Chicago Press, 1951).

Glock, Charles Y., "Afterword: A Sociologist Looks at the Parish Church," in Walter Kloetzli, *The City Church; Death or Renewal: A Study of 8 Urban Lutheran Churches* (Muhlenberg Press, 1961).

Glock, Charles Y., and Roos, Philip, "Parishioners' Views of How Ministers Spend Their Time," *Review of Religious Research,* Vol. 2 (Spring, 1961), pp. 170–175.

―――― "Religion and the Integration of Society," *Review of Religious Research,* Vol. 2, No. 2 (Fall, 1960), pp. 49–61.

―――― "The Sociology of Religion," in Robert K. Merton, Leonard Broom, and Leonard S. Cottrell, Jr. (eds.), *Sociology Today: Problems and Prospects* (Basic Books, Inc., Publishers, 1959).

Goode, William J., "A Theory of Role Strain," *American Sociological Review*, Vol. 25 (August, 1960), pp. 483–496.

Greeley, Andrew M., *The Church and the Suburbs* (Sheed & Ward, Inc., 1959).

Greenblatt, M., York, R. H., and Brown, E. L., *From Custodial to Therapeutic Patient Care in Mental Hospitals* (Russell Sage Foundation, 1955).

Gustafson, James M., "The Clergy in the United States," *Daedalus*, Vol. 92 (Fall, 1963), pp. 724–744.

—— *Treasure in Earthen Vessels: The Church as a Human Community* (Harper & Brothers, 1961).

Harrison, Paul M., *Authority and Power in the Free Church Tradition* (Princeton University Press, 1959).

Herberg, Will, *Protestant—Catholic—Jew: An Essay in American Religious Sociology* (Doubleday & Company, Inc., 1955).

Justice, John C., "Report on Factors Related to Membership Growth of United Presbyterian Churches Organized January, 1950, Through December, 1959" (mimeographed paper, Institute of Strategic Studies, 1963).

Kraemer, Hendrik, *A Theology of the Laity* (The Westminster Press, 1958).

Lenski, Gerhard, *The Religious Factor* (Doubleday & Company, Inc., 1961).

McCarroll, Richard S., *A Guide for the Development of a New Church* (The United Presbyterian Church in the U.S.A., 1960).

Marty, Martin E., *The New Shape of American Religion* (Harper & Brothers, 1958).

—— *Second Chance for American Protestants* (Harper & Row, Publishers, Inc., 1963).

Michels, Robert, *Political Parties: A Sociological Study of the Oligarchical Tendencies of Modern Democracy*, tr. by Eden and Cedar Paul (Free Press, 1949).

Moberg, David O., *The Church as a Social Institution* (Prentice-Hall, Inc., 1962).

Musselman, G. Paul, *The Church on the Urban Frontier* (The Seabury Press, Inc., 1960).

Nash, Dennison, and Berger, Peter L., "The Child, the Family, and the 'Religious Revival' in Suburbia," *Journal for the*

Scientific Study of Religion, Vol. 2, No. 1 (Fall, 1962), pp. 85–93.

Niebuhr, H. Richard, *Christ and Culture* (Harper & Brothers, 1951).

—— "The Norm of the Church," *The Journal of Religious Thought,* Vol. 4 (1946–1947), pp. 8–15.

Niebuhr, H. Richard, in collaboration with Williams, Daniel Day, and Gustafson, James M., *The Purpose of the Church and Its Ministry: Reflections on the Aims of Theological Education* (Harper & Brothers, 1956).

O'Connor, Elizabeth, *Call to Commitment* (Harper & Row, Publishers, Inc., 1963).

O'Dea, Thomas F., "Five Dilemmas in the Institutionalization of Religion," *Journal for the Scientific Study of Religion,* Vol. 1 (October, 1961), pp. 30–39.

Parsons, Talcott, "General Theory in Sociology," in Robert K. Merton, Leonard Broom, and Leonard S. Cottrell, Jr. (eds.), *Sociology Today: Problems and Prospects* (Basic Books, Inc., Publishers, 1959).

—— *The Social System* (Free Press, 1951).

—— "Some Ingredients of a General Theory of Formal Organizations," in A. W. Halpin (ed.), *Administrative Theory in Education* (The University of Chicago Press, 1958), pp. 40–72.

—— "Suggestions for a Sociological Approach to the Theory of Organizations," *Administrative Science Quarterly,* Vol. 1 (1956), pp. 63–85, 225–239.

Parsons, Talcott, and Shils, Edward A. (eds.), *Toward a General Theory of Action* (Harper & Row, Publishers, Inc., 1962).

Robinson, John A. T., *et al., Layman's Church* (Alec E. Allenson, Inc., 1963).

Schuyler, Joseph B., S. J., *Northern Parish* (Loyola University Press, 1960).

Selznick, Philip, "An Approach to a Theory of Bureaucracy," *American Sociological Review,* Vol. 8 (February, 1943), pp. 47–54.

—— "Foundations of the Theory of Organization," *American Sociological Review,* Vol. 13 (February, 1948), pp. 25–35.

Selznick, Philip, *Leadership in Administration: A Sociological Interpretation* (Row, Peterson & Co., 1957).

―――― *TVA and the Grass Roots: A Study in the Sociology of Formal Organization* (University of California Press, 1949).

Shippey, Frederick A., *Protestantism in Suburban Life* (Abingdon Press, 1964).

Sills, David L., *The Volunteers: Means and Ends in a National Organization* (The Free Press of Glencoe, 1957).

Thompson, James D., and Bates, Frederick L., "Technology, Organization, and Administration," *Administrative Science Quarterly*, Vol. 2 (December, 1957), pp. 325–343.

Thornton, Martin, *Pastoral Theology: A Reorientation* (London: S.P.C.K., 1956).

Tillich, Paul, *The Protestant Era*, tr. by James Luther Adams (The University of Chicago Press, 1948).

Vance, Robert R., "An Analysis of Procedure and Policy Changes Suggested by First Ministers of Churches Organized 1950 to 1959" (mimeographed paper, Institute of Strategic Studies, 1963).

Whyte, William H., Jr., *The Organization Man* (Doubleday & Company, Inc., 1957).

Wilson, Bryan, "An Analysis of Sect Development," *American Sociological Review*, Vol. 24 (1959), pp. 3–15.

Winter, Gibson, *The Suburban Captivity of the Churches: An Analysis of Protestant Responsibility in the Expanding Metropolis* (Doubleday & Company, Inc., 1961).

Wurster, Catherine Bauer, *Housing and the Future of Cities in the Bay Area* (Institute of Governmental Studies, University of California Press, 1963).

Yinger, John M., *Religion in the Struggle for Power: A Study in the Sociology of Religion* (Duke University Press, 1946).

INDEX

DATE DUE

AUG 8			
MAY 5			
MAR 25			
GAYLORD			PRINTED IN U.S.A.